W9-BLU-205

Help 4 NonProfits & Tribes

BASIC 4 TRAINING ★★ NON PROFITS
★★★★

Workbook Series

Renaissance Press • Tucson, Arizona

www.Help4NonProfits.com

Help 4
NonProfits
& Tribes

CAPACITY BUILDING RESOURCES AND CONSULTING
★ Board Development
★ Strategic Planning
★ Marketing
★ Web Strategy
★ Sustainable Fund Development
★ Feasibility of New or Expanding Programs

BASIC 4 TRAINING NON PROFITS
★★★★ ★★

Board Recruitment and Orientation

A Step-by-Step, Common Sense Guide

by
Hildy Gottlieb

Renaissance Press • *Tucson, Arizona*

Board Recruitment and Orientation
A Step-by-Step, Common Sense Guide
by
Hildy Gottlieb

Published by:
Renaissance Press
P.O. Box 13121
Tucson, Arizona 85732   U.S.A.

Orders@Help4NonProfits.com
http://www.Help4NonProfits.com
1-888-787-4433

All rights reserved. No part of this book may be reproduced or transmitted in any form or by any means, electronic or mechanical, including photocopying, recording or by any information storage and retrieval system, without written permission from the author, except for the inclusion of brief quotation in a review. Neither the author nor the publisher guarantee the success of any of the steps contained herein, which steps are provided as suggestions only. Both author and publisher disclaim the likelihood of success of any of these steps and accept no liability nor responsibility to any person or entity with respect to any loss or damage, caused or alleged to have been caused directly or indirectly by the information in this book.

Unattributed quotations are by Hildy Gottlieb

Copyright © 2001 by Hildy Gottlieb
Photography by Art Clifton, A C Productions
Workbook Design and Artwork by Dimitri Petropolis

ISBN: 0-9714482-8

Library of Congress Control Number: 2001095707

Dedication

To NonProfit board members everywhere, who do their job simply because they care about their world. I salute you.

Acknowledgments

Putting together a book is a big task - I never knew how big until I tried it. Now I understand why just about every book starts out by thanking people. It sounds cliche, but really and truly, an author can't do it alone. And so the following people are here in these pages as well.

Hank Lewis, Nanette Pageau and Dyan Petropolis read my first-draft manuscript and didn't tell me to "keep my day job." For that, and for the input they gave in that early stage and along the way, I thank them. Same goes to Dick Onsager and Steve Nill, who helped me clarify the finer legal points in the book.

Walt Nett is a great friend and a great editor. I never thought anyone could make it fun to edit my own work. Thanks, Walt. And to Phyllis Updegrave, who spent the holiday weekend proofreading, you are the best.

Thanks must go to Sue Myal, whose willingness to share her experience and wisdom from the publishing world has been invaluable. And to Art Clifton, who played enough ZZ Top to get this horribly camera-shy writer to jump in the air and smile for the camera. My mom, Rose Gottlieb, and my brother and sister-in-law, Marty Gottlieb and Jeri Slavin, encouraged me to keep at it. That means a lot.

There are three people without whom I couldn't function, whether writing a book or simply remembering to breathe. Nanette Pageau is the very best friend anyone in the whole world could have. She made this book happen and makes my life happen and I love her a lot.

Lizzie Sam is my daughter and my hero. She shows me that life is amazing, every single day, and I couldn't be more inspired by anyone.

And my business partner and best friend, Dimitri Petropolis. Your artwork and your sense of the ridiculous make people actually want to read my words. You put up with me every day and think that's just fine. Your faith in me, your encouragement, your support - you are such a huge part of why this book is actually here. There aren't words enough to say what that means to me.

Finally, I must thank my colleagues on the Charity Channel lists. Every day I learn from you and grow from you. Every day you make me think of things in different ways. You all make me better at what I do, and for that I cannot thank you enough.

With the warmest sincerity,

Hildy

Contents

Step 5:
Preparing the New Board Member to Govern   99

OVERVIEW: 100

Afterwords   113

PREFACE
★★★★★★★★★★

Who We Are and Why We Wrote This Book

The last thing any of us has these days is time to waste on a bad book. Personally, before I invest much time in a "business" book, I want to have a pretty good sense of whether the book will help me to be better at my work or simply waste my time.

And so, before going much further, I thought you might want to know a bit about my business partner, Dimitri Petropolis, and me; our business, **Help 4 NonProfits and Tribes;** and our reasons for producing this book, to help assure you that the time you invest in reading it will be well spent.

Dimitri and I live and breathe the NonProfit world. We have worked as consultants exclusively to NonProfits and Native American Tribes for going on 10 years, doing everything from board development to fund development; from strategic planning to marketing planning; and points in between. We've taught workshops across the U.S. and published articles in NonProfit-oriented journals ranging from the obscure to the Chronicle of Philanthropy.

We have also, along the way, founded a NonProfit in our own community, one that is about to grow to a statewide organization. And so our perspective comes from both inside and outside the NonProfit walls.

Neither of us set out initially to be NonProfit gurus. We started as two individuals with strong political and business backgrounds, who happened to land at the same real estate firm; who refocused that firm towards business turnaround and eventually bought the company.

Frustrated that our "day jobs" had little long term meaning, and finding ourselves spending more and more volunteer time sharing our business and political skills in the NonProfit world, we decided, once again, to refocus the company. But this time, we didn't have a plan - just a goal. We wanted to know that at the end of the day, our work had had some positive impact on our world.

It wasn't long before **Help 4 NonProfits and Tribes** was born.

We have been blessed, since that time, to have spent our days helping organizations as varied as an environmental NonProfit in a Mexican fishing village; an Indian tribe trying to make tourism work where gaming could not; and a rural health clinic trying to plan its future on the edge of a growing city. We've spent months with a tiny Indian tribe trying to grow its economy from within, and a child abuse shelter trying to nurture delicate changes in its board.

Our work in this arena has made us passionate about increasing the effectiveness of NonProfit organizations, because the better they are at what they do, the more improvement we will see in our communities and our world. And those end results are really all that matter.

So Why This Book?

In our travels, we've had hundreds of conversations with NonProfit CEOs and Board Members. And if we were to pick the single overriding theme of each of those conversations, it would be "Frustration."

Running a NonProfit isn't easy. And while there exists a plethora of self-help books and organizations to assist business leaders, there is little out there for leaders in the NonProfit world. Nor are there a lot of models for "doing it right."

Board Members complain about the scarcity of training materials for doing their job well. They tell us (and we've seen in practice) that so much of the materials that do exist conflict with the reality of a volunteer board that is trying its best and yet still feeling like they're just not getting it right. CEOs face the same frustrations, only they live it every day - it is their job to live it.

Folks outside the NonProfit world are prone to say that NonProfits should learn to "operate like a business." But in practice, solutions that work in the business world often don't work in a NonProfit setting. A NonProfit's goal is not to MAKE money, but to USE money as a tool to achieve a higher purpose. Although they must run efficiently and be prudent with their dollars, NonProfits are not businesses. They are fiduciaries, acting on behalf of those who donate their money to make their communities better. It is an awesome responsibility.

The results NonProfits are seeking are different than those sought by a business. So are the things that keep NonProfit leaders awake at night. It makes sense that the approach to solving those problems therefore be different as well.

As people who've re-dedicated their lives to helping NonProfits create positive change, we wrote this book to help you get around the obstacles and head straight for the results. To accomplish that, we know the book has to be practical and usable, and to some degree fun. We hope we've succeeded in all those areas.

Because in the end, results are really all that matter. By making your organization healthier and more effective, your community will benefit.

And at the end of the day, Dimitri and I will feel good if we've had some small part in that.

Introduction

"Think of the worst board member you've ever known, and remember that someone actually recruited him."

Why a Strong Recruitment and Orientation Program is Important

As NonProfit consultants, we talk to a lot of board members. Given the degree to which those board members whine about their boards, sometimes you'd think they were complaining about their spouse or their job!

When it comes to boards, we hear words like *"dysfunctional"* or *"ineffective."* Board members complain that

"Meetings are too long"

"No one shows up for meetings - we can't even get a quorum."

"Meetings are boring."

"One person commandeers every discussion to no real end. We are so relieved when he's absent."

"Our board micromanages every detail."

"Not our board - we just rubber stamp everything staff's already doing."

A study cited in the Wall Street Journal a number of years ago asked organizations the following question:

If your board was abducted by aliens,
would the organization notice they were gone?
Would anyone pay to get them back?

Given this frequently well-deserved attitude towards the boards we sit on, is it any wonder we feel desperate to find new board members? Good ones this time, not like that jerk we finally got rid of. Folks who can help us stay on track. Folks who can help us make it all work.

> *But come on - those people will never sit on our board. We're just a small __fill-in-the-blank___ agency, not some powerful group. We'll never have the good board members - they're all sitting on those high-profile boards. We had trouble even attracting the people we have now! Everyone is so over-committed these days. We're lucky to get who we get.*

If any of these laments sound familiar, then you're in luck. The good news is, it's fixable. The better news is that you can fix it yourselves.

A strong recruitment and orientation program is a key piece in your efforts to create a more functional board. Through effective recruitment, you will gain control over who sits on the board, and you will stop feeling desperate to accept whoever walks in the door. Through effective orientation, you will prepare those new board members to serve from the moment they've arrived.

Syndicated columnist Dale Dauten recently cited a study on employment success. The study showed that of all the factors one might think would impact employment success, the single most important factor was "fit." It seems the more time a candidate spends with the firm's members **before he/she is hired**, the closer the fit once they are hired. "Fit" was the single best predictor of both job satisfaction and tenure.

The recruitment and orientation process should set the stage for a great "fit" for your board members. The process alone will tell potential board members a lot about the way the board approaches its job within the organization.

And so, our wish for you is simple - the whole reason we've created this workbook:

> When the aliens come for your board members,
> we want your organization to immediately notice they're gone.
> And we want them to pay handsomely to get those board
> members back.

What This Book is About

Ask 10 organizations about their recruitment and orientation process, and most will either answer with only a chuckle or define their process as follows:

"We give names to the nominating committee, and they contact the individuals and ask them if they would like to serve on the board. The prospect attends a board meeting to see what their job will be, and then at the next meeting, we vote them in."

"Our orientation process? We give them a ton of materials on the organization in the board manual. Then they attend board meetings until they figure out what committee they want to sit on."

If your organization is like most we hear about, you spend more time, money and energy recruiting and training your janitorial staff than you do in preparing a new board member for their new job.

We forget that recruiting new board members is really hiring and training people to do a job - the critical job of monitoring and guiding the organization to ensure ongoing benefit to the community. Leadership. Governance.

So how can we make sure we recruit the right people and prepare them well for the job ahead?

The answers can be found in the following steps:
1. Define the job clearly (both the job of the board and the job of the individuals on the board)
2. Recruit good people
3. Give them the tools they need to do the job
4. Measure board members' performance (the performance of both the board and the individual board members)
5. Remove those who don't measure up

This workbook will focus on the first three of these factors:
- Defining the job duties of individual board members
- Recruiting good people
- Giving them the tools they need to do the job

Resources to help you with the remaining steps, including defining the role of the board (the other part of #1 above) can be found in the Afterwords, at the end of this workbook.

A Note About the Role of the Board

It is difficult to do a good job of recruiting and training board members when the board itself is uncertain of its job. A strong recruitment and training program will not improve the performance of a dysfunctional or wayward board. On the contrary - it could lead to high turnover and a sour taste in the mouths of those you recruit.

In the Afterwords of this workbook, you will find questions to help you determine whether or not your board is ready to recruit new members. We strongly advise that the creation of a recruitment and training program be part of a larger plan to develop your board into a cohesive group, focused on governing and bringing your organization and your community into the future.

When all these pieces are in place, your organization will be ready to make incredible positive change on behalf of the community you serve.

How to Use this Book

The process outlined in this workbook is complete, comprehensive - and may be a big plunge for your organization. Done as a comprehensive unit, this workbook is enough to keep your board development committee busy for a full year - maybe two!

So take it a step at a time. Use some of it, and save the rest for later, when you're ready for more.

Or choose just the parts that seem right for your board's needs.

There is no one right way. Do what's best for your board, given your particular circumstances.

All these methods are tried and true. But they don't all have to be adopted at once, and they don't all have to be used together.

Any steps you take to enhance your recruitment and orientation efforts will be a big step towards improving the performance of your governing board.

So take the plunge. What are you waiting for?

Recruiting and Training New Board Members

THE 5 STEP PROCESS

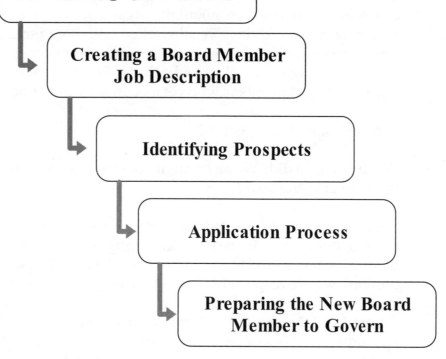

Establishing Qualifications

Creating a Board Member Job Description

Identifying Prospects

Application Process

Preparing the New Board Member to Govern

A STORY

Someone Recruited Them
or
The Thing that Wouldn't Leave

When John Belushi was on Saturday Night Live, he would do a sketch about a boorish houseguest who just would not go home. They called the sketch "The Thing that Wouldn't Leave."

Ever feel that way about a board member?

We've all worked with board members who are so domineering and out of line that they make board meetings intolerable. We've all worked with board members who care about the organization, but can't seem to show up for meetings. And we've all worked with board members who show up at every meeting, but never say a word and never serve on a committee, so they might as well never be there! Board members with their own agendas. Board members who get meetings off onto unbearable tangents.

Who recruited these people?

We did. We all did. We all thought, for whatever reason, that they would be an asset to the board.

We all have war stories, but the part we forget is that we are responsible for their being there in the first place. Any of us who have sat on a board, made a motion to accept a nominee onto the board, voted to approve that motion - we are responsible for "The Thing That Wouldn't Leave."

Throughout the rest of this book, we will show you situations we have encountered. These case studies are real, but these are sensitive issues, and so we've changed the names of groups and individuals for the sake of their anonymity.

As you read these stories, we hope you will think about your own stories. And every time you think it seems like too much work to use a process for recruitment - when you think it would just be easier to do it the way you've always done it - we encourage you to remember your own "Thing that Wouldn't Leave." And suddenly, all that effort will seem worthwhile.

"There is no end to what you can accomplish if you don't care who gets the credit."

Florence Luscomb, suffragist

Step 1:
Establishing Qualifications

"Warm Blood and a Pulse"

Establishing Qualifications

★ Creating the "Must Have" List
★ Creating the "Wouldn't It Be Nice" List
★ Creating the "Never In a Million Years" List

Creating a Board Member Job Description

Identifying Prospects

Application Process

Preparing the New Board Member to Govern

OVERVIEW:
What are you looking for?

Whenever we help boards develop a recruitment program, we start by asking the group what they are looking for in a board member. And without fail and only half in jest, someone will pipe up with, "Warm blood and a pulse."

I say "only half in jest" because one look at some of their board members will tell you that this has indeed been their selection criteria!

You can't find the right people to lead your organization if you don't know what you're looking for. Step One, therefore, is to establish criteria for selecting board members, so you'll know when you've found the right person.

There are 3 steps to determining the desired qualities for your board members:

1. Creating "Must Have" criteria
2. Creating "Wouldn't It Be Nice" criteria
3. Creating "Never in a Million Years" criteria

Once you have established what you are looking for, you will be well on your way to writing a job description for your board members. You will also have criteria against which you can measure their application, their interview, and their performance.

CHAPTER 1

★★★★★★★★★

★★★★★★★★★

"Must Have" Criteria

The "Must Have" criteria are not what you might initially think. They are not deep pockets, great connections or the desire to donate pro bono work.

The "Must Have" criteria are those traits you wish everyone on your board had - the things that will make or break your board's ability to carry out its job. And because the primary job of a Governing Board is to govern, your "Must Have" criteria will be those qualities that make for a great governing board.

Joe is a great fundraiser, but he is domineering and won't be part of any group where he can't have his way. Chances are Joe will be a flash in the pan - he'll raise some money quickly, make board meetings a nightmare, leave in a huff and cause the board a long period of healing after he's gone.

Who needs it?

One way of defining the "Must Have" criteria is to ask: If our organization was 100% funded and money were no option, what would we look for in a board member?

Notice what's not on that list, once you think of it that way. Personal wealth. Donated professional services. These may be things that would help the organization as a whole, but they are not the things most critical for board members. They are not the things that, if lacking, will leave the board unable to guide and monitor the organization.

But what is on the list is what really affects how boards function. Here are some possible examples:

✪ Positive, can-do attitude

✪ Understanding of our community and its needs

✪ Passion for our cause

- ✪ Willingness to commit time for board meetings, committee meetings, planning sessions, special events

- ✪ Team player - works well in a group and is willing to set aside ego for the greater good

- ✪ Someone who listens well, is thoughtful in considering issues

- ✪ Someone who is interested in leading and governing, rather than simply volunteering or doing a portion of the day-to-day work of making the organization function

- ✪ Someone who can see the forest for the trees, understands the big picture of the community's need for the mission of the organization.

- ✪ Willingness AND ability to add their expertise, time, resources when the need arises - not already overcommitted

The list will differ for each organization, and will change as the organization changes.

BRAINST☆RM - "Must Have" Criteria

Use this sheet to brainstorm with your board (or Board Development Committee) what characteristics you feel your board members MUST HAVE.

"Must Have" Characteristics of Board Members for Our Agency

© 2001 Help 4 NonProfits & Tribes
www.help4nonprofits.com

★★★★★★★★

CHAPTER 2

★★★★★★★★

"Wouldn't It Be Nice" Criteria

Wouldn't it be nice if we could find someone who was all the things we wanted in our "Must Have" list and who also had the wherewithal AND willingness to donate $1million per year to our organization?

The "Wouldn't It Be Nice" list is all those other qualities you'd like to find in a board member AFTER they've passed the "Must Have" test.

"Wouldn't It Be Nice" traits are those you wish at least SOMEBODY on your board had. Maybe you even wish a few people had these traits. But it really isn't necessary that everyone have these traits. This list will include those specific skills and talents, areas of expertise, contacts, etc. that would be terrific cream.

The operative word here is NECESSARY. Is it NECESSARY that every board member have a particular skill? Then it's a "Must Have." Otherwise, it would just be nice.

These qualities will vary from board to board, and will change over time. For example, the Finance Committee may be looking for someone with financial savvy. The public relations committee may need someone with those special skills. A health clinic may want a board member who is a client of the clinic, or possibly a board member with knowledge of the medical field. A child care center may want someone with expertise in early childhood development.

Most boards we have worked with had not a single board member with expertise in the organization's mission. Medical facilities, food banks, public broadcasting. And they have been very successful. We've also seen boards who DO have that level of expertise in one or two of their board members, and they too have been successful.

And the reason that level of skill isn't needed for the board is that the board's role is NOT to perform the day-to-day work. Its role is to guide and monitor - to govern.

And so the "Wouldn't It Be Nice" criteria are really "in addition to" criteria. They are not critical when it comes to the ability to govern, but for at least a few folks, it would sure be nice.

I'm Confused

This is the point where at least one person in a training group will raise their hand and say what's probably on the mind of half the room.

> *"I'm confused. I've always thought we need rich people on the board, and experts in the field. I've thought we needed lawyers and accountants and folks who will do free work for us. And now you're telling us that none of this is necessary?"*

A good way to look at the difference between what you really NEED on the board and what would simply be nice to have is to consider the search for a spouse.

Your husband, wife, significant other.

Wouldn't it be great to find a mate who was wonderful to be with AND rich?

But now let's say you have to choose - you can have rich, or you can have wonderful to be with. Which will it be?

For most people, the answer is clear. It is critical to have someone with whom we mesh. If they had money, it would be nice. But for most of us, given the choice, we'd rather have the person that will make our lives pleasant.

And the same goes for your board. The critical factor is not the depth of their pockets, but the depths of their character. If Susan is a decent caring person who wants to help guide the organization, it is unlikely that Susan's inability to donate large sums of money will create a board that is unable to govern. But if Susan can't work as part of a team, can't leave her ego at the door, can't think of the best interests of the community - Susan's presence on the board will be a hindrance, regardless of how much money she has.

Establishing qualifications is about acknowledging that first things come first. Those are the qualities your board members Must Have. And all the rest would just be nice.

WARNING:
★★★★★★★★★★★★

Before You Add the Words "Pro Bono Attorney or CPA" to the "Wouldn't It Be Nice" List, Read This!

There are attorneys who make great board members. There are CPA's and PR people who make great board members. And that only happens when they are NOT on the board in their professional capacity. These professionals must be on the board to govern, and not to provide pro bono work. Period.

There are three reasons you should NOT seek pro bono professionals for your board.

First, board members are there to govern, and not to do the work that should be staff and/or volunteer work. As John Carver says in his groundbreaking book, Boards That Make A Difference , "The board is responsible for creating the future, not minding the shop."

However, most boards that set out to recruit a CPA do so to make up for a lack of adequate financial expertise on staff. They hope that a CPA on the board will straighten out their bookkeeping systems and keep an eye on the finances, all for free, for the whole 2 or 3 year term of their board appointment.

What really happens, though, is that the CPA stops thinking like a board member - "creating the future." Instead she is thinking like a staff person, watching day-to-day management issues and procedures, adding her expertise where she feels things are not up to her standards. She starts "minding the shop" because that's what she's been asked to do.

When we put a CPA on the board to help with the finances, we can't complain when they micromanage - we've asked them to! The same applies to any professional who is invited on the board to act as pro-bono staff.

The effect of the management-focus of a pro bono professional is not just the loss of one board member. One pro bono professional on the board can wreak havoc on the focus of the entire board, as other board members will defer to that professional under the assumption that "she's in the trenches, so she should know." We've seen whole boards unravel from the participation of a single pro bono professional.

The **second** reason applies mostly to attorneys who sit on boards as pro bono lawyers. By providing legal counsel to the board at the same time as being a member of that board, the attorney will have a direct conflict of interest - advising the board on legal issues that will ultimately protect him as an individual. For this reason it is a bad idea for an attorney to take on this role, as there is no way to do this cleanly.

The **third** reason to refrain from using board members as pro bono professionals has to do with logic and business sense, because it is unlikely that you will find a professional whose practice centers around the issues specific to NonProfit organizations.

What does a medical malpractice attorney know about NonProfit law? Will he be conversant in Intermediate Sanctions and private inurement issues - the things that land individuals in court and NonProfits in newspaper headlines? Will that CPA be well-versed in UBIT issues (Unrelated Business Income Tax) that can affect how your organization raises funds? Does the PR person who represents the tire store and the beer distributor understand that NonProfit marketing must communicate different messages to at least 2 distinct audiences?

When we look for specific skills on our "Wouldn't It Be Nice" list, we are not looking for pro bono staff people. These positions are sirens, luring you to the rocks with a sweet song in the short term and danger in the long term. The skills you seek should allow the board to do the work of governing at the highest possible level. Board members with these skills must be there to lend their expertise to help the Board govern, and not to help the staff manage. Period.

ESTABLISHING QUALIFICATIONS

BRAINST★RM - "Wouldn't It Be Nice" Criteria

Use this sheet to brainstorm with your board (or Board Development Committee) what qualities or skills would be nice to have on the board, in addition to the "Must Have" criteria.

We'll kick off the list with just one entry, the obvious one. The others will be more specific to what it takes to adequately guide and monitor your particular organization.

"Wouldn't It Be Nice" Characteristics of Board Members for Our Agency
1) Wealthy and willing to donate / well-connected to friends who will donate

© 2001 Help 4 NonProfits & Tribes
www.help4nonprofits.com

★★★★★★★★★

CHAPTER 3

★★★★★★★★★

"Never in a Million Years" Criteria

An important part of the process of determining what you want is to determine what you DON'T want.

> If the "Must Have" list includes traits you wish *everyone* on your board had, and the "Wouldn't It Be Nice" list includes traits you wish at least *someone* on your board had, then the "Never In a Million Years" list will include those traits you *never* want to see on your board.

Some of these will already have come up in your discussions, as you've thought about the traits that could unravel your board under the "Must Have" category.

The "Never in a Million Years" criteria fall into three areas.

1. The first is general qualities. We don't want someone quarrelsome. We don't want a big ego. We don't want someone domineering. Etc. These are the easy ones, because they are pretty much the same for every group. The hard part is using these criteria to disqualify candidates, especially when those candidates were recommended by a board member! ("I'm sorry, Jane, but your friend Richard failed on the ego/domineering scale.") But in the end, these are the qualities that can tear a board apart if they aren't taken into consideration in the screening process.

2. The second area of concern should be those individuals who are interested in joining your board as a way of advancing their own business interests. Some people consider NonProfit board participation as a just another business networking meeting - lots of other professionals with whom to exchange cards. There are also those who hope to engage the organization itself as a client, leading to all sorts of potential for conflict of interest. It's not always easy to uncover this motivation, as most folks won't readily confess such intentions. By including this in your "Never in a Million Years" criteria, you will be more aware of clues that indicate that a prospect only wants to join your board for their own personal / professional advancement. Further, setting policy that specifically excludes this behavior sends a clear signal to both current and future board members.

3. The third area covers those issues that are specific to your board. These issues will probably arise on a case-by-case basis, and you will probably add to or take away from the list over time. Again these issues can be covered by policies, applied consistently.

For example:

✪ How do you feel about married couples or people who are otherwise related sitting on your board? What if both are active in the community and great finds?

✪ How do you feel about former employees sitting on your board? What if they've just been fired?

These criteria will be specific to your organization, because what is great for one organization may be disaster for another. The following example is extreme, but it proves the point:

✪ How do you feel about having a convicted rapist on the board of your center for abused women and children? Would that be different if the organization was a re-entry agency for sex crimes offenders leaving prison?

Many of these criteria will arise in the normal course of the board's business. Be attentive to them and create policies to deal with them. Apply those policies consistently to ensure they are effective and enforceable.

WARNING:

Regardless of whether or not the letter of the law would apply EEO rules to NonProfit boards, it is bad PR and bad practice in general to use these criteria as an excuse to discriminate. In these enlightened times, using any policies or practices to keep protected classes from sitting on your board (or participating in any other activity) is not just potentially illegal and morally reprehensible, it is bad business and not very smart. If you are in doubt about whether or not your policies could be viewed as discriminatory, check with a Human Resources attorney (yes, even for your board) and remember the adage - when in doubt, don't. Diversity makes for a better board and a better organization overall.

BRAINST✪RM - "Never in a Million Years" Criteria

Use this sheet to brainstorm with your board (or Board Development Committee) what qualities you want to avoid.

"Never in a Million Years" Characteristics of Board Members for Our Agency

© 2001 Help 4 NonProfits & Tribes
www.help4nonprofits.com

Warm Blood and a Pulse

Rural NonProfits frequently have a hard time finding good board members. The population base is small to begin with, and the same people seem to sit on every board. Finding board members that reflect the diversity of the population further complicates matters.

One group we worked with had such a hard time finding good people that they would appoint to the board anyone who was willing to serve. When we asked their criteria for "hiring" board members, they said it - "Warm blood and a pulse."

The result, though, was a board headed for disaster. First, there was the constant complaint that they just couldn't find good board members - people who really care and really want to serve the community and the organization. Board members didn't show up for meetings, and frequently there was no quorum, an insult to those who rearranged their schedules and traveled some distance to make the meetings. As a result, turnover was an ongoing issue, and much of the board's time was spent searching for board members, just to maintain the minimum number required by their bylaws. The board was almost always filled with new people, just learning their way.

When we were introduced to this board, they were virtually unable to govern. Of the 15 board members on record, NONE of them had been on this board for longer than a year, and almost none had toured the facility. Many had only a vague notion of what the organization really did, and others had no sense of the deep impact the organization had had on the community. One board member had joined thinking he could gain the agency as a client for his insurance business.

One of the first steps we took in helping this board find its way was to help the organization define what it wanted from its board members. What kinds of people were they looking for?

The following was their "Must Have" list:

✪ Knows the community and has a genuine concern for what's best for the community

✪ Works well in a group

✪ Listens without taking sides

- ✪ Willing to make the time commitment
- ✪ Has common sense
- ✪ Hard worker / Dedicated
- ✪ Honest
- ✪ Can take criticism (had been an issue, as the board was trying to change certain group behaviors that had become institutionalized)
- ✪ Ability to keep focus on the big picture / refrain from micromanaging
- ✪ Reflect the ethnic diversity of the community

It is easy to see that most of these criteria were pretty universal, while some were specific to issues that had arisen for this board at this time.

The group's "Wouldn't It Be Nice" criteria were surprisingly NOT focused on money, but connections. This board was more concerned with getting things done in the community than with the ability to bring in money. Again, the criteria suited their own specific needs.

Through attrition, board seats became available. Those who stayed had a lot in common - they cared, knew the community, and wanted to work hard. And when it came time to look for replacements for those who had left, the board set out to look for folks that fit their new criteria.

The results were energizing for a couple of reasons. First, it is exciting to have board members who are, in a sense, prequalified. But more important, simply by establishing these criteria, the board began to take control of its future. They no longer felt they needed to take whoever walked in the door. This small step of empowerment had ripples throughout all the rest of their recruitment and orientation efforts.

"Experience is not what happens to a man. It is what a man does with what happens to him."

Aldous Huxley

Step 2:
Board Member Job Description

"I had no idea what I was getting into"
or
"You expect me to do WHAT?"

Establishing Qualifications

Creating a Board Member Job Description

★ *Job Purpose / Objective*
★ *Job Duties / Responsibilites*

Identifying Prospects

Application Process

Preparing the New Board Member to Govern

OVERVIEW:
Job   Description

Most people picture job descriptions as something used for employees. And so when we ask to see job descriptions for board members, usually we get a look of confusion or disbelief. Unlike some of the other items in this workbook, where boards know they should have it but just don't, frequently boards never even think of having a job description.

The purpose of a job description, regardless of the job, is to make sure that expectations are clear. Being a member of your board is a job. The job descriptions for your NonProfit board members will therefore be used for exactly the same purposes they would be used for paid employees - to make your expectations clear.

The following are standard elements of an Employee Job Description. Not surprisingly, they all apply to board members as well!

- ✪ Purpose / objective of the job
- ✪ Job duties / responsibilities
- ✪ Skills / qualifications required to do the job
- ✪ Hours required
- ✪ Special training required

You will notice that you've already figured out the skills and qualifications you are looking for. After reviewing the job duties, you may have more items to add to your "Must Have" and "Wouldn't It Be Nice" lists.

As you make it easier for your board to recruit good people, a job description will be a great tool for clarifying both your objectives and those of your prospective board members.

★★★★★★★★★
CHAPTER 4
★★★★★★★★★

Job Purpose / Objective

What is the purpose of having board members? Why bother? (And no, the answer isn't "Because state law and our bylaws require it.")

The purpose of having board members is to provide direct links between the community and the organization - to provide continuity. Having community representatives guide and monitor the organization is the way to keep the organization accountable to the community, within the context of its mission and vision. Is the organization working to provide results to the community? That act of monitoring and guiding to ensure those results is the reason board members are needed.

Pretty hefty responsibility, eh?

The job of board member is to act in a fiduciary capacity. Fiduciary means that you are acting on behalf of someone else, to protect their best interest. And so the role of board member is to protect the best interest of the community by monitoring and guiding the organization.

If we were talking about a FOR profit corporation, we would say the board of directors has a fiduciary duty to the stockholders. In a NonProfit organization, the "stockholders" are the general public. They are the ones who benefit from your organization's success. They are the ones who donate in the hopes that the community will be better off.

And so the purpose of having individual community members on the board is to make sure the best interests of the community are represented. The only way that can happen is if board members acknowledge their obligation to monitor and guide the organization in the direction of the public's best interests.

And the word that best summarizes "monitoring and guiding" is the word "governing."

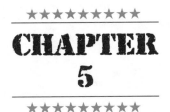

CHAPTER 5

Job Duties / Responsibilities

So what, then, are the duties and responsibilities one must perform in order to adequately govern the organization and represent the interests of the community?

Attend board meetings? Participate in those meetings? Educate themselves so they can, in fact, participate?

Participate in committees? Help raise funds?

> To avoid viewing all these tasks in a vacuum, it is important to place all the board's activities in the context of the purpose defined on the previous page - to represent the community's best interests. And so, for example, you are not expected to attend board meetings for the sake of attending meetings, but for the purpose of monitoring and guiding the organization in the direction of the public's best interests.

That perspective provides a lot to brainstorm! What are your board's expectations as you try to fill the role of guiding and monitoring the organization to represent the community's best interests?

The following are a sampling of job duties often written into board member job descriptions. Not all will necessarily apply to your organization, and you may have some that are not on this list, that are specific to your organization.

- ✪ Attend and participate in board meetings - regular meetings, special meetings, annual planning sessions - to monitor and guide the organization's progress in obtaining results for the community.

- ✪ Attend and participate in committee meetings, to monitor and guide the organization's progress in obtaining results for the community.

- ✪ Participate in the organization's special events, both as a representative of the community, and to provide support.

- ✪ Prepare in advance to make educated decisions, through review of materials, discussions, etc. to monitor and guide the organization's progress in obtaining results for the community.

✪ Avoid, and where impossible to avoid, disclose conflicts of interest.

✪ As the link between community and organization, not only represent the community to the organization, but also to represent the organization to the community, acting as an ambassador for the organization.

✪ Always act with prudence and ethics, adhering to the values and the policies of the organization, and putting the best interests of the organization (and therefore the community) before your own.

✪ Continually educate oneself on those issues related to the mission of the organization, to monitor and guide the organization's progress in obtaining results for the community.

✪ Resign if you find you cannot perform these duties.

Again, not all these will apply, and your organization may have some specific needs that are not listed. But this is a good start for brainstorming the job duties that will help your board members fulfill their role as the link between the community and the organization.

BRAINSTORM - Job Description

Job Title:

(*Member, Board of Directors ABC Organization*)

Job Purpose:

(*Represent the best interests of the community by governing (monitoring and guiding) the organization towards its vision and mission.*)

Job Duties:

(*Brainstorm your own list of job duties.*)

Qualifications:

(*Use your own list of criteria, and add any that come to mind, now that you're thinking in this light.*)

Special Training:

(*Note if there is any special training needed for board members. This kind of item sometimes appears in highly specialized fields such as medical groups, etc.*)

Hours Required:

(*List the hours required for board meetings, committee meetings, special meetings, planning retreats, etc.*)

© 2001 Help 4 NonProfits & Tribes
www.help4nonprofits.com

You Expect Me to Do WHAT?

We were working with an organization based in our hometown, whose work extended into two countries. During their search for board members, they decided to ask someone they considered highly qualified. She was bright and giving, well connected, pleasant and responsible. In addition, she would bring a lot of professional skills to the board.

I know all this because the woman they chose happened to be my best friend!

My friend called to ask my opinion, because she knew I was working with this group. She already sat on a number of boards, was newly married, and was trying to scale back, rather than add more. She was considering this board for two reasons. One, she had heard from me what a great organization it was. The second reason, though, was that they had told her all she'd need to do was attend board meetings for an hour each month. So what did I think - should she do it?

We won't get into the ethical hard place this put me in. I chose to tell her I was busy and couldn't talk right then, and called the Board President. I reminded him of all the work the organization was doing and how involved the board was with that work. I reminded him of their realities:

✪ That their board meetings were rarely short of 2 hours

✪ That they had hoped new board members would be active on at least one committee

✪ That at least one meeting per year is held outside the country over a 3-5 day period, where board members were expected to pay for their own transportation

Yes, I know, my friend would have been a real find. And they didn't mean to lie or dupe her into being on the board. The truth was simply that the person who had approached her hadn't thought it through.

By providing a prospect with a job description, you aren't relying on the perceptions of whoever is making the pitch. The reality of the job is right there on paper, making it easier on both the prospect and the person approaching him/her about the job.

A woman comes upon a young man searching around under a street light. "Can I help you find something?" she asks. "I've lost my keys," he answers.

"Where did you last see them?" she asks. "Over there," the young man answers, and points across the street to a dark corner.

"If you lost them over there, why are you looking over here?" the woman asks.

The young man looks at her incredulously and answers, "Because this is where the light is."

Old Traditional Fable

Step 3:
Identifying Prospects

"Is your pool of prospects as big a pool as the last time you hired a janitor?"

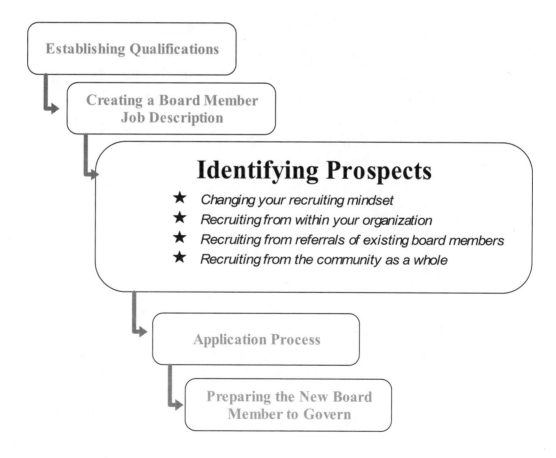

Establishing Qualifications

Creating a Board Member Job Description

Identifying Prospects

★ *Changing your recruiting mindset*
★ *Recruiting from within your organization*
★ *Recruiting from referrals of existing board members*
★ *Recruiting from the community as a whole*

Application Process

Preparing the New Board Member to Govern

OVERVIEW:
Where do we find good prospects?

When we ask folks "Where have you found prospects in the past?" they hem and haw.

- ✪ They tell us they have trouble finding people to serve.

- ✪ They tell us that the Nominating Committee will come up with a few names for the seats they have open, and that they will then approach those people to serve. Depending on the number of seats they have open, they will probably prioritize an order in which they'll ask, based on who they'd like best. "We'll ask George, and if he says no, we'll ask Larry."

You've established qualifications, so you know what you want. Now where do you find them?

The steps in identifying prospects are intended to provide you with the broadest range of choices possible. Those steps include:

1. Changing your recruiting mindset
2. Recruiting from within your organization
3. Recruiting from referrals of existing board members
4. Recruiting from the community as a whole

Once you have a pool of recruits, the application process will truly become the time when you choose your board members, rather than hoping they will choose you.

★★★★★★★★★

CHAPTER 6

★★★★★★★★★

Changing Your Recruiting Mindset

Lets look at two scenarios:

A NonProfit needs to recruit a janitor. They place an ad, screen a dozen or more resumes and applications, interview 2 or 3 individuals and hire the best one.

A NonProfit needs to recruit a board member. They come up with 2 or 3 possible names from existing board members, ask each if they'd be willing to serve. Whoever says 'yes' is in.

It's easy to see why board recruitment goes this way. But the problem is not "out there" with our prospective board members. The real problem is inside us. It is our perceptions and perspectives about both our organization and the recruitment process.

Watch:

Perspective A

NonProfit board members are giving their time. Good people are already over committed, with the same people sitting on all the good boards. The best board members sit on high profile boards, not boards like ours. We're so small and insignificant compared to those big boards. And so it's unlikely those good board members will want to help with our board.

Perspective B

Our organization and our board do such amazing things! Our board members are so enthused and excited about the work we do that they talk about this organization everywhere they go! People in the community come to us - they want to help and would be honored to have the opportunity to serve on our board. And so we always have a pool of great people to choose from, any one of whom would be terrific.

If your board is like most boards, you immediately identify with Perspective A - that desperate feeling that resigns itself that things will always be this way, because that's just the way it is. This sense of desperation puts full control of the recruitment process into the hands of the prospect, because, to quote the characters in the movie Wayne's World, "We're not worthy."

So the first step in identifying prospects is to change your mindset about both your board and those prospects.

Your goal is not to find just one candidate who can please, oh please, fill that one seat you have available.

Your goal is to maintain a pool of prospects who would love to help your terrific organization in any way they can.

If you have 10 seats open, recruit for them as if you were recruiting for one at a time, finding a pool of candidates for each seat. Or maybe decide that you will fill 3 of those seats, taking the top 3 candidates from that pool, and then waiting a few months to see if you can fill the pool up with more great prospects. Or maybe take any candidate that scores 8 or higher on their interview. ("Scoring? What's that?" you ask. Just wait!)

The bottom line is to stop thinking in desperation and to start recruiting for your governing board from the same position of strength that you recruit for your janitor.

So How Will You Create this Pool of Prospects?

There are three main sources for finding prospects:

★ Look for prospects from the existing volunteers within your organization

★ Look for prospects from referrals of current board members

★ Look for prospects from everywhere else

Who Should Look for Prospects?

By now it should be pretty clear that the job of recruiting board members belongs to the board. But the truth is that in many organizations, that is not the way it goes.

In many organizations, the CEO recruits board members. After all, the CEO comes into contact with supporters of the organization all day long. And no one knows the organization like the CEO.

Further, in some organizations, the CEO not only searches for prospects, but interviews them and provides recommendations to the board. Those boards are generally stacked with members with whom the CEO feels he or she can work.

How many bad practices does this scenario lead to? How about the following as a start:

- ✪ Virtually all bylaws of all NonProfit corporations state that the CEO is hired and fired by the board, serving at the board's pleasure. For the CEO to choose his/her supervisors is a direct conflict of interest.

- ✪ A problem experienced by many boards is that feeling of serving simply as a rubber-stamp for what staff recommends. The logic in these organizations goes as follows: Because board members are only volunteers, they must rely on the staff to provide technical background for their decisions. The issue of rubber-stamping is only exacerbated when the CEO has, in effect, hand chosen the board.

For a myriad of reasons, it is a bad idea for the CEO to do your board's recruiting. If the CEO finds a likely candidate, that person should be suggested to the Board Development committee, from which point the CEO should have little further to do with the process. (The best place for CEO input is outlined in the following section.)

This all comes back to the need for the Board to understand its role in the organization, and the responsibilities that stem from that role. Specifically, it is essential that the Board understand how its role relates to the roles of the staff. For more information about roles and responsibilities, see the Afterwords section on page 113.

★★★★★★★★★
CHAPTER 7
★★★★★★★★★

Recruiting from Within Your Organization

In their groundbreaking book, _Built to Last_, James C. Collins and Jerry I. Porras discuss the qualities that keep visionary companies a step ahead of the rest. One of those qualities is the preference for hiring from within.

Even in small organizations with a small staff and few volunteers, you will often find the people you really want to hire are already there, proving themselves every day - demonstrating their loyalty and their skills and their passion for your mission. This holds true whether you are hiring staff or "hiring" your board.

The best way to allow a prospective board member to develop and demonstrate commitment to your mission, and to get a feel for the way your organization functions, is to recruit them first as volunteers. Some organizations create a process where prospects from outside the organization are encouraged or required to sit on committees or volunteer in some other manner first, and then board members are recruited from that volunteer pool. Other organizations have less formal mechanisms, simply looking to their existing volunteers first, before going outside the organization to recruit for the board.

Regardless of how strict you are about requiring board members to have volunteered first, your choice of new board members is more likely to be a success when you recruit from within.

A word of caution, though. Don't let the fact that you "know" this person stand in the way of using the criteria to determine if they really fit the job. This is the one downfall to choosing from within - the tendency to relax standards because this person is a friend.

Gathering a List of Prospects

The following will be a helpful exercise to get a good list of prospects. It can be used for any of the recruitment scenarios in this section.

For The Board

Consider doing this exercise with the whole board, rather than just the Executive or Board Development Committees, simply to increase the number of potential candidates.

1. At a board meeting, take a few minutes and have each board member list 2 people (or 3 people, or even one person) they know who might be a good prospect for the board. Make sure they have the qualifications criteria in front of them as a reminder.

2. For every person on their list, have them note what qualities their prospects have that match the criteria. This will focus them away from "I don't know anyone with money" and focus them onto "Sue has been so energetic and passionate about our mission as a volunteer."

3. Make this an agenda item and have board members work on this list right there at the board meeting. You don't have to make it any more than a 5 minute exercise. Depending on how well people know each other, they might break into groups to brainstorm names. This works when they know each other well and can suggest folks for another person, as in "What about Mary? Don't you work with her on the playground committee? What do you think of her abilities?"

If they want more time to think about it and suggest taking the sheet home, give them another sheet for that purpose. But if you don't get a list from them right then and there, you are less likely to get it later. It's worth the 5 minutes of board meeting time to make sure it gets done.

For Staff

If it makes sense within the construct of your organization, go through this same exercise with staff at a staff meeting. The venue will differ, depending on the organization. In some organizations, only management staff or volunteer supervisors should suggest candidates. In other venues, the folks most likely to know volunteers intimately may be line staff. Use your judgement for determining who should come up with the list of names, and whether this exercise is appropriate for staff at all.

Have the staff do the exercise in the same way - listing not only the name of the person, but the qualities that would make them a good board member. And again, have the work done while they are sitting in the staff meeting, to be sure it gets done.

BRAINST★RM - Prospects from Within Your Organization

Names of potential board members, from existing volunteers / committee members AND why they would make a good board member.

Potential Board Member List	
POTENTIAL BOARD MEMBER	DESCRIBE QUALIFICATIONS

© 2001 Help 4 NonProfits & Tribes
www.help4nonprofits.com

CHAPTER 8

Recruiting From Individuals Suggested by Existing Board Members

If you have no qualified volunteers from which to create a pool of prospects, having existing board members propose names is the next best method for recruiting. This is the method used by most boards. It works well because your board members know the job, know the organization, know the criteria, and will be in a good position to pre-screen those who might be good candidates.

Use the same approach as you used on the previous page. Do the exercise at the board meeting, so board members can brainstorm and get a list together right then and there.

IDENTIFYING PROSPECTS

BRAINST★RM - Prospects from Existing Board Members
Names of potential board members from existing board members

Potential Board Member List	
POTENTIAL BOARD MEMBER	DESCRIBE QUALIFICATIONS

© 2001 Help 4 NonProfits & Tribes
www.help4nonprofits.com

★★★★★★★★★

CHAPTER 9

★★★★★★★★★

Recruiting from the General Population

What happens if you've looked throughout the organization and still don't have a big enough prospect pool? How do you keep the pipeline filled with prospective volunteers and board members?

The answer is to constantly watch for folks who want to help.

There are two steps that are guaranteed to find people who want to serve the mission of your organization. The first is to look in places you haven't looked before. The second is to invite them to get excited about your organization's mission and vision, and to see the good work you are doing to realize that mission.

Step One - Looking in New Places

If you were looking for a new administrative assistant - someone who could take over the parts of your life that you just can't handle yourself - you would probably tell everyone in the world that you were looking. You'd announce it at networking meetings. You'd ask your friends. Does anyone know of a great administrative assistant?

The same holds true for board members. Here are some places to start:

✪ In public speeches on behalf of the organization, let the crowd know that you are always on the lookout for good people who want to serve as volunteers or board members.

✪ In breakfast clubs, networking groups, etc., when you have the opportunity to make announcements, ask for folks interested in helping the agency by serving or volunteering.

✪ Advertise in your organization's newsletter, on your website - wherever you are asking for assistance.

✪ Contact your town's newspaper. Many papers run free "volunteerism" listings.

✪ Talk to your local United Way, community foundation, volunteer center, or other large NonProfit whose mission is to help the NonProfit community, and let those leaders know you are looking.

✪ Talk to people who talk to people. Your community's religious leaders. City or Town Council members.

Step Two - Invite them to Get Excited

Once you have people interested, invite them to tour your facility with you (or the CEO, or a knowledgeable and energetic staff person). You might consider setting up regular tours (every 1st Monday, for example), where interested parties can see firsthand what your organization is doing for the community.

If you don't have an exciting facility, you can set up presentations, talking about the work you accomplish and the need that remains unmet.

Getting people excited about the work your organization is doing is the best way to get them to commit their time, their money, and their hearts.

Picture This:

You've announced at your breakfast club (or church group or Rotary, etc.) that there will be a tour of your organization for anyone interested in what the group does. You have let them know up front that this is NOT a fundraising gimmick - that they won't be asked for money (their main fear). You have told them you just want the community to know what amazing things the group is doing. You followed up with the people who showed interest to remind them a few days before the tour.

The day of the tour, only 3 people show up. But by the end of that tour, those three people are jazzed! They had no idea your group did this amount of work! They would love to help in any way they can!

Now you not only have 3 prospective volunteers or board members, but you have 3 more people out there telling folks what a great morning they had and what great work you are doing!

BRAINST✪RM - Recruiting from the General Population

Places you (as an individual could look for / announce board member needs.

Places to Look for / Announce Board Member Needs

© 2001 Help 4 NonProfits & Tribes
www.help4nonprofits.com

Approaching Prospects

One of the biggest ways we get ourselves into trouble in the recruiting process is the way we approach potential candidates. Regardless of which method you use for identifying prospects, when it comes to approaching that candidate, you will want to avoid the following trap.

George, I'm on the XYZ Agency Board. Would you consider being on our board?

This approach comes from that feeling of desperation, that feeling that's still willing to settle for warm blood and a pulse. It comes from not knowing quite what to say. But it also opens a whole boat load of expectations - primarily the expectation that the board has invited this person, and so they are as good as "in."

Now lets try a different approach:

George, I'm on the XYZ Agency Board. We are talking to a number of prospects for the board seat we have open, and you've been mentioned as a great prospect. Our recruitment process has a number of steps, including an interview with the Board Development Committee. Would you consider putting in an application?

This approach eliminates some of the awkwardness in not choosing a particular candidate. They haven't been promised anything, so there is no need to feel you must "uninvite" them.

Why People Don't Approach Boards to Serve

It's true that it is not common to have people knocking down your doors to serve on your board. Part of the reason is that people ARE pressed for time and already committed to other groups.

And part of the reason has to do with the simple function of being asked. Generally, people see sitting on a board as something one must be invited to do.

JoAnne was the liaison from a company that was sponsoring an event for the Save the World Society. She attended all the sponsor meetings, and along with other sponsors, was invited to tour the facility and learn more about the great work Save the World was doing.

JoAnne was the kind of prospect boards dream of. She was bright and funny, had great common sense and no ego issues - a real team player. The more she learned about the organization, the more she loved the work they did. She'd already proven herself through her sponsorship role, and she wasn't overcommitted with other boards!

When it was suggested that JoAnne be approached as a board member, the board president responded that JoAnne was so familiar with the organization that if she were interested, she would have said something.

Well a board member talked to JoAnne anyway. And JoAnne was honored and touched that the board would think she was qualified to help in that way! She thought board members had to be high up in their profession, that they had to come from a certain strata of society. She had never pictured herself as board material, and would never have presumed to approach the board to suggest herself as a member. She felt that would have been conceited of her!

Some people think you can only get onto a board (especially a more prestigious board) if you are well connected.

Some people think that being a board member takes special skills, or the ability to raise large amounts of money, and they don't feel they have those skills.

Some people feel it would be somehow conceited to suggest they might be of value. "Who do I think I am to suggest myself to them?"

And some people just want to be asked.

And so most people wait to be approached.

You can change that simply by letting people know it's not so. Get out and tell the world - your board is looking for help!

Your Best Recruiting Tool

One of the best recruiting tools is a board that is alive and focused. Like a club everyone wants to join, it will be easier to attract great prospects if the work your board is doing is phenomenal and your existing board members are jazzed.

With a board that is excited and energized, your existing board members can be the bridge between Scenarios A, B and C. Their talking about the organization will make strangers into friends. Their touring those strangers / friends through your facility, or talking to them over lunch about the amazing work your organization is doing, will be an introduction that folks won't be able to forget.

When highly energized board members approach their own list of prospects and invite them to take a tour, to learn about the organization and its vision and mission, those prospects feel that energy. They want to be part of it.

And you will see that pool of prospects growing before your eyes!

A STORY

No Pool of Prospects

The Do Good Group had never had any luck finding candidates for its board. They had been around for 30 years, and their founder was still CEO. He was also still their chief recruiter, doing recruitment the same way he had done it 30 years ago - asking just about anyone he met if they were interested in serving. Next thing you knew, those folks were attending a board meeting and being voted in. These individuals came and went, and the organization often faced an insufficient number of board members per their bylaws.

That was the situation when Do Good was asked to provide their services for the employees at the local manufacturing plant. The CEO met with Hank, the plant manager, and by the time the meeting was over, he had asked Hank to be on the board. After all, Hank was a manager, a professional. And he was willing to serve!

The honeymoon lasted about as long as Hank's first board meeting.

Hank, it seems, was a tyrant. The people who worked for him hated him. Hank also had never been on a NonProfit board before, and so the only skills he could fall back on were those he used in his role as manager at the plant. He began to micromanage everything, because that's what he knew - management.

After two months, Hank started gunning for the CEO, insisting that he could run the place better with both eyes closed. It was at that time the CEO and the Board President called in a consultant. (That would be us.)

The work we did included helping the board grow beyond the founder's ways of doing things, as the founder wanted to retire and wanted to be assured that the organization would continue to provide its great service to the community after he was gone. The more the board worked on its basic structure and roles, the more excited they got about everything the organization did and could do.

Except for Hank. Hank hated what was happening. And a short time into the project, he quit in a huff. You could feel the board sigh with relief. It had been the worst few months any of them had ever endured.

The board was so excited about their new role in the organization that they couldn't wait for their long term planning session. At that session, they vowed to use Do Good's mission to make the community a better place. And they couldn't wait to get to work.

Now their energy as a group precedes them wherever they go. They talk about the organization at church and at Rotary. They talk about the board at work and when they are chatting with friends. They are so excited about the work they are doing that they talk about it all the time.

And slowly, folks are coming to them. For the first time in the history of the organization, the board is full and they have a list of prospects for when terms expire. Those prospects have their applications in, and while they await new board terms, they are volunteering to help in other ways. The board can pick and choose from these qualified prospects, and the energy continues to grow.

It took a lot of work, but in a way, Do Good has Hank to thank for all of it. Hank was the last one selected without a pool to choose from, the last one recruited by the CEO. And now, they can't imagine ever doing things that way again.

"The truth of the matter is that you always know the right thing to do. The hard part is doing it."

General H. Norman Schwarzkopf

Step 4:
Application Process

"Getting to Know Each Other"

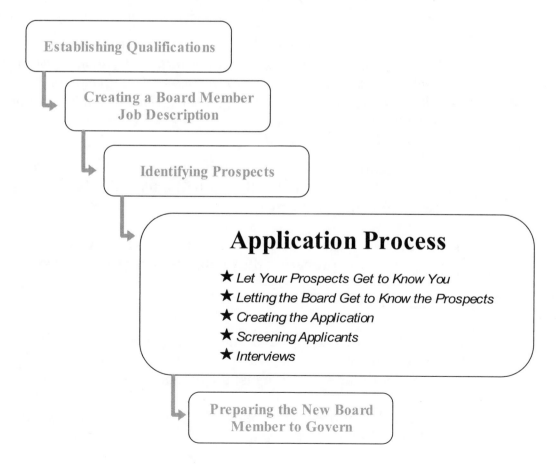

Establishing Qualifications

Creating a Board Member Job Description

Identifying Prospects

Application Process

★ *Let Your Prospects Get to Know You*
★ *Letting the Board Get to Know the Prospects*
★ *Creating the Application*
★ *Screening Applicants*
★ *Interviews*

Preparing the New Board Member to Govern

OVERVIEW
The Application Process -
Getting To Know Them as They Get to Know You

Do we have to go over the horror stories of the standard NonProfit board application process? You ask them to be on the board, have them attend a meeting, vote them in, and no one really knows if this is a good fit!

Let's look behind the scenes:

Joe is on the board of the Dynamic Agency. He has suggested Felicia as a board member. She's in his Rotary, and he thinks she'd be great. He suggests her to the group, and they invite her to sit in on their next board meeting, which she does. Now it's time for the board to vote her in.

Jane is another board member for the Dynamic Agency. She has been on another board with Felicia, and Felicia did nothing. If she doesn't want to offend Joe, she won't say anything. If she's a bit bolder, she might say something to the person next to her. And if she's really bold, she might say something publicly, at the table.

But regardless of what Jane does, nobody else knows Felicia but Joe and Jane. The board ends up speculating, spending twenty minutes debating whether or not Felicia might have had other reasons for being a less-than-exemplary board member at the other organization. They agree that she seemed nice when she visited the board meeting last time. The board decides to give Felicia the benefit of the doubt, and they vote her onto the board.

We've all been through this. Try and think back - has there ever been a nominated board member that you can recall, that had attended a board meeting and then NOT been voted onto the board?

Well, by now we know there has to be a better way. And you've already done most of the legwork - preparing the qualifications, gathering a pool of candidates.

Now what?

Now it's time to get to know these new candidates, to let them get to know you, and to see if there's a fit. In this way, there will be a whole group of people who get to know the candidates, and not just the one person who proposed his/her name.

This is where all that prep work pays off. As they say in the car commercials, this is where the rubber meets the road.

The application process has 2 major components:

- ✪ They get to know you
- ✪ You get to know them

They will get to know you via an introduction process and then through the interview.

You will get to know them via applications and again, through their interview.

By the time you are done with the application process, not only will you sense if the fit is right, but so will your prospective board members.

WARNING # 1:
★★★★★★★★★★★★★

A Word About the Application Process

The process we are about to outline is probably different than you are used to - more complicated, more involved. More and more organizations are turning to this type of process, as they are sick of getting bad board members to join their boards.

Until more people are used to this as the standard, though, you will find candidates who object to "jumping through hoops" just to sit on a board. "No other organization in town makes me go through this! Do you have any idea who I am? I'm in demand!"

The answer to these folks, and to anyone who is skeptical about this process, is that board members and the board as a whole are legally liable to govern well. Just one example of this is the institution of regulations by the IRS on Intermediate Sanctions, which make individual board members, as well as the board as a whole, personally and collectively responsible for actions that result in excessive or unjustified personal gain for one or more board members.

Board members are fiduciaries - parties acting on behalf of someone else - the community. And governing towards the future of this organization and the future of your community is so important that your board must be sure there is a fit - and that the people you choose are the ones you really want.

And the others? There are other options for how they can help, and they are detailed on page 123 in the Afterwords.

But as for making the commitment to responsibly govern your organization, a prospective board member who "refuses to jump through hoops" may be telling you something about his/her commitment simply by those very words.

WARNING #2
★★★★★★★★★★★★

Be Consistent

The important thing in the application process is that you set a process and stick to it. Making exceptions is not fair to the applicants and will come back to bite you some time down the road.

Decide to interview every candidate. Or decide to interview every candidate that scores a 10 or better on their application. Or decide to interview the top 4 applications. Whatever.

Just make sure that during a single round of recruitment, that you always do it the same.

Whether the purpose of going outside the process is to benefit a certain candidate, or to eliminate a certain candidate is irrelevant. Stick with the process you have decided upon for ALL candidates, applying the same standards consistently.

Aside from not being fair to the applicants whose time you have taken for this process, an unfair process will wreak havoc on your organization. Imagine being a board member who proposed one of the candidates that didn't get in through this manipulated process! The consequences could be an angry board member, a whole angry board, the potential for lawsuits, bad PR and, if any of your board resigns, even more board seats to fill (not to mention all the other damage control).

So don't do it. Go through the same process with everyone.

★★★★★★★★★

CHAPTER 10

★★★★★★★★★

Let Your Prospects Get to Know You

The Introduction Process

Most prospective board members know very little about the organization they are being asked to govern. Even if they have been a faithful volunteer, they are generally unfamiliar with those aspects of the organization that fall outside their specific work area, and even less about the workings of the board itself.

And so while they are in the application process, they should be given a good sense of what they are getting themselves into. Providing some form of introduction process before someone is appointed to the Board helps them determine if they even want to be on the board!

There are three questions you will want this process to answer:

1. What is this organization all about?
2. What would my job as board member be?
3. How does the recruitment process work?

The introduction could be as comprehensive as having them attend a board meeting, tour the facility with a senior staff person and chat informally with a board member just to answer questions. Or it could simply be a 20 minute video or a brochure. However you do it, let this person know what's behind the organization they may be leading.

Board Member Introduction

What is the organization about?

Providing your mission statement is not enough. Try to remember what it was like when you were a new board member - what would you have liked to have known? (Some board members don't feel like they know the organization even after sitting on the board for a year. If that's you, what would you like to know now?)

A brief summary of your programs and funding sources? The organization's long range and short range goals? (Remember - if you want a prospect to get excited about working with your organization, your long range vision speaks volumes.) Information on the bottom line results to the community?

Again, it is important to note that just because someone is already volunteering, they will most likely not have this kind of knowledge about the whole organization. It is safest to assume that your prospects know nothing, and to work from there forward.

This information could be provided in a brochure or a video, or it could be done in a tour of the facility by a staff person or board member (or both). Items such as newsletters are also helpful.

What would be my job as board member?

Let your prospects know what will be expected of them. Provide them with a copy of the board member job description you've created. Let them know how much of a time commitment it will require to be on this board. Let them know what role the board takes in the organization - what the board does for the organization.

In addition to the job description, a brochure or video works here as well. Informal chats with board members (or, depending on the group, a group Q&A session) can work for this purpose as well.

How does the recruitment process work?

Give them the overview of what to expect from your process AND how you will decide whether or not they will be chosen to sit on the board.

> Tell them they will fill out an application.

> That their application will be reviewed along with the applications of the other candidates.

That if they pass that level, they will be provided with a tour of the facility or a video or whatever it is you want to do to pass along information to them.

That there will be an interview.

That if they are chosen to be on the board, there is an orientation program that will allow them to hit the ground running.

Etc.

Whatever your process is, let them know that the process is intended for them to know you, as well as for you to know them - to see if there is a fit.

This is easily handled in a brochure, a video, or a personal conversation.

APPLICATION PROCESS

BRAINST★RM - Creating the Introduction Process

The most important question here isn't "Should we do a video or a brochure?" The most important question is "What information do we want to convey?"

To accomplish this, jot down your answers to the following questions. What information do you think is important for someone to know in each of these categories? List everything you can think of.

1) What is this organization all about? Why does the organization exist? What does it do?

2) What is my job as board member all about?

3) How does the recruitment process work?

© 2001 Help 4 NonProfits & Tribes
www.help4nonprofits.com

An Example of an Introduction Piece:
The Recruitment Brochure

Your introductory information may fit on a single brochure or fact sheet. Obviously a brochure won't tour folks around the facility, but it can begin to give them a comfort level with your organization.

You might try a question and answer format, as it's readable and helps you get right to the point. You might consider writing it from the perspective of the new board member "What if I'm new to board work?" That personal approach is a good way to let them know you are interested in them as a person - that you are thinking about their interests, and you understand that they have questions. After all, in addition to giving them factual information, one reason for creating this piece is so prospective board members will feel great about serving on your board!

Join the ABC Crisis Nursery and Shelter Board of Directors and Help Us Build a Safer Community For Our Kids!

Vision and Values
The long term vision of the ABC Crisis Nursery and Shelter is a safe community for our children. In making decisions at ABC, the most important value is the safety of our community's children.

What does ABC do?
ABC Crisis Nursery and Shelter provides ....

What is the board's role at ABC?
The ABC board is a governing board, providing policy and leadership to the organization....

What will be expected of me as a board member?
Board members are expected to attend and participate in board meetings (one meeting per month, on the last Thursday of every month). In addition, board members are expected to serve on at least one board committee...

I've never been on a board before. Is there training for me to get up to speed?
ABC has an extensive orientation program to help you find your place in our organization....

What is the process for getting on the board?
Governing our organization is one of the most critical roles someone can play at ABC. That's why we recruit a pool of potential board candidates for every seat on the board. The process is simple - .....

And so on - explaining all the things they need to know (or at least what can logically fit into a brochure). This brochure, along with a copy of the Board Member Job Description, provides a simple introduction to the organization and the process of becoming a board member. Add a tour or a chat with an existing board member, and your prospects will have a good sense of what life will be like with your organization!

CHAPTER 11

Letting the Board Get to Know the Prospects
Applications and Interviews

The purpose of the application is to begin to know something about your prospects. Do they have any of the qualities you said you were looking for? The application will be your first clue - their first introduction to the board.

Applications and interviews should ask questions that immediately get to what you want to know about the prospect. They should center around your list of qualifications - your "Must Have" and "Wouldn't It Be Nice" lists.

If the only reason you can find for a question to be on the application is because it's always been there, scrap it. Don't waste your prospect's time with anything you don't really want to know. This will be especially important during the interview, when we tend to ask all kinds of bizarre questions just because we think we're supposed to, or that these questions will somehow reveal the person's inner soul. "If you were stranded on a desert island..." should NOT be the start of an interview question unless your NonProfit is a desert island rescue team. And the same is true for the application.

★★★★★★★★★

CHAPTER 12

★★★★★★★★★

Creating the Application

Creating applications is simple, because you already have all the pieces - now you'll just put them all together.

First, do not expect an application to reflect a lot about your prospect. The qualities you've listed in your "Must Have" and "Wouldn't It Be Nice" lists are not the kinds of things one can easily discern from an application.

Keep the application simple and short - as non-intimidating as possible. Try and keep it to one side of one page. If there is that much more you want to know, save much of it for the interview. The application will give you the most basic of information, because most of what you want to know is what a person is really like, and that's hard to put onto an application.

The kinds of questions that belong on an application are those that can be answered with quantitative answers (Have you ever sat on a board before? Do you have experience reading a financial statement? Do you have time to commit to this organization?) rather than qualitative answers (What do you like best about sitting on a board? Why are you interested in joining our board?). Yes/no answers are great on an application, or at the very least, answers that can be given in one line.

Don't make someone write an essay - let them quickly tell you about themselves in light of what you want to know.

Now here's the important part:
After you've decided on the questions, determine what answer you want for each of them. This will make it far easier to move the process forward.

Application Questions:

Keeping to questions that can be answered in a very short answer, what kinds of simple quantitative questions can we ask to find out about our "Must Have" and "Wouldn't It Be Nice" Criteria?

The following are examples of the thinking that can generate questions for your application:

Example Questions	Desired Answer
Do you have experience sitting on a governing board? What other boards do you currently sit on? ★ *(This not only talks to experience, but lets you know if they're already committed to 5 other boards!)*	What answer would you like to see here?
If you do have experience on a board, what committees have you participated in? Have you participated in any other special board activities besides board meetings? ★ *(Find out what they've done on those boards!)*	What answer would you like to see here?
What special skills would you bring to this board? ★ *(What do they think is important and/or special about themselves? Is it one of your "Must Have's"? Could it maybe even be one of your "Never in a Million Years" criteria?)*	What answer would you like to see here?
Our board meets monthly for approximately 2 hours. Most committees also meet monthly, for approximately 2 hours. In addition, every May we take 5 days out of town for a planning session. Are you able to commit this amount of time to meetings and the other work necessary in governing this organization? ★ *(Self explanatory)*	What answer would you like to see here?

And remember - most of the questions that really get to know a person are best asked during an interview, and NOT on an application. If some of the criteria just can't be figured out in a simple one or two word answer, save those for the interview and concentrate on the simple things in the application.

APPLICATION PROCESS

BRAINST★RM - Application Questions

For each of your criteria brainstorm a question that can have a brief answer, for the application.

Questions	Desired Answers

© 2001 Help 4 NonProfits & Tribes
www.help4nonprofits.com

CHAPTER 13

What Do You Do Next?

Ok, they've filled out the application. What's next?

It is important to note again that whatever process you choose for decision-making and screening, you should be consistent in how you apply that process.

That said, the next decision is how you want to screen these applicants.

Do you want to see if their application has some red flags that tell you that you don't even want to interview them? Do you want to assign points to each of their answers and only interview those with the highest number of points? Do you want to just use the application as a baseline of information for asking more questions during the interview?

Once you decide which path to take, stick with it for every candidate during this round of recruitment, to be sure everyone is treated fairly.

If You Choose to Screen Based on the Application

Sometimes you have so many candidates for so few board seats that it doesn't make sense to interview all of them. And sometimes, you have placed critical "deal breaker" questions on the application that will make or break a candidate's chances of being on the board.

In these cases, you will want to screen the applications, to determine who moves on to the interviews.

When we screen, we have a tendency to make it far more complicated than it needs to be. The following method is meant to be simple and fair.

1. Using a chart format, for each relevant question, write down what the answer was supposed to be. Then put a column to the right of that, and check off whether or not their answer was the "right" one according to your scale. Check mark means "yes, their answer was what we wanted." No check mark means their answer didn't measure up. If you're not sure, put some code for that as well.

2. Do the same for all your critical questions.

3. Total up the check marks to determine their total score.

4. Decide what score will qualify someone to be interviewed.

We prefer to recommend using the "yes they have it" or "no they don't" approach, rather than ranking someone on a scale of 1-5, because applications are cold flat creatures that leave lots of room for interpretation. They don't give the prospect the ability to clarify, to answer a follow up question, or to say what they really mean. So all you can do is to say, "well, it looks like they've got it" or "it looks like they don't."

And one more thing - when in doubt, give them the check mark. That's where the "I'm not sure" code can come in handy. It may mean you interview one more person, but that's worth the benefit of the doubt.

The Time for CEO Input

The previous section made pretty clear that it is a bad idea for the CEO to be the board's chief recruitment officer.

There is, however, a critical place for the CEO to provide limited input, and that place is right here.

The following question should be posed to the CEO, once all the applications are in:

> *Are you aware of any material factual information that any of the applicants omitted or failed to disclose in full, which would be relevant to our decision?*

Given the degree of influence many CEOs have over board decisions, phrasing the question in this way makes it clear that you are not looking for "soft" answers, such as "I'm not sure I will feel comfortable working with him." Some of the best board members we have ever encountered do not have comfortable relationships with the CEO, and that adds to the value they bring to the group.

Instead, the question ferrets out serious factual issues that can sabotage all the good work your board is trying to do. For example, "I fired Larry two years ago, when he worked for me at ABC Group. His last words to me were 'I'll pay you back if it's the last thing I do!'" This is pretty relevant stuff!

Because of the inherent conflict of interest in a CEO influencing the choice of who sits on the board, the recruitment process must remain primarily a board process. But when it comes to relevant facts, the CEO must have input or the board could be missing essential information upon which to make its ultimate decisions.

★★★★★★★★★

CHAPTER 14

★★★★★★★★★

The Interview

Lets go back to the first page of this section, page 72, where we talked about the fact that the application process has two parts:

They get to know you, and you get to know them

Nowhere is this more the case than during the interview. If your interview is done right, your candidates will get as much out of it as you will! Stress the "inter" part of the word interview, and you can't lose.

And so you will want to let your candidates know this before the interview - that the purpose of the interview isn't just so you can interview them, but for you to interview each other. Tell them to bring all their questions about the board, the organization, their role on the board - bring all of it to the interview.

At the same time, this will be your chance to get to know your candidates to see not only who will best fit onto your board, but where they might fit in.

There are three steps to finding out what you want to know from the interview:

1. Create the questions

2. Determine what you want the answers to be

3. Create a ranking system for scoring the candidates

The interview team should consist of 2 or 3 board members, no more.

Make sure the interview is conducted in a setting where everyone can feel comfortable to ask and have their questions answered. For whichever candidate you eventually choose, this interview will be your first step to becoming a team!

Creating Interview Questions

To interview well, you will start at the same place you started for the application - the qualifications. Now is the time to ask all those things that just didn't fit on the application.

Would you describe yourself as a team player or do you prefer to lead the pack?

What do you think you will like best about being on this board? Where do you think you would best fit in? What kinds of board tasks do you like best?

Have you ever been on a board that's had internal board problems? How did you handle that? What did you do?

At work, is your style more likely to delegate to others or to do it yourself?

Just follow your criteria and ask what you really want to know. Throw in some of the "Never in a Million Years" things too, if you want - whatever makes you comfortable in finding out how this person will fit in.

Obviously, because this will be a two-way street, a real conversation, you will want to leave room for spontaneous questions (so long as you don't ask the one about the desert island!). But make sure you ask the things you really want to know, and the only way to do that is to create the questions ahead of time and ask everyone those same questions.

Predetermining Desired Answers

This is the step that takes a lot of the stress out of interviewing. (As an aside, this is a good technique to use in interviewing paid employees as well.)

Once you know what the questions will be, know what answers you're looking for.

For example:

At work, is your style more likely to delegate to others or to do it yourself?

If you are looking for someone who can delegate, then "delegate" is the right answer. If the candidate says, "I find that if you want something done right, you have to do it yourself," then you can note that he got that answer "wrong."

Create a chart similar to the one you used for the application (see sample on next page). In the first column, you'll put the question, as well as the desired answer. In the second column, leave room for a check-mark if they answered it appropriately. And in the third, leave room for comments and/or notes.

First, list your "Must Have" questions, and leave a line for a sub-total. **All** these questions should have answers before they are asked. Then list the "Wouldn't It Be Nice" questions, leaving a line again for a sub-total.

Leave room for writing in those "Never in a Million Years" things that you notice. Angry? Uncooperative? Bossy? Make sure you provide evidence of those traits if you see them - just telling the group "He seemed angry to me" isn't going to be enough.

During the interview, use this sheet as your notes sheet for each candidate. Check off the answers they get "right" and leave that space blank for the ones they get "wrong." If you want to, take notes on why you answered that way and move on to the next question.

And if someone rambled on and on and you couldn't tell whether or not they answered the question, they probably didn't. And they will probably ramble on and on that same way at board meetings!

SAMPLE INTERVIEW FORM

MUST HAVE Questions (with Desired Responses)		COMMENTS
Do you Delegate at Work? Yes, I believe in delegating	X	Talked a lot about giving people the freedom to do their job.
Have you Been on a Board with Problems? I helped the board heal		There was a problem because the staff would never do what I told them to do and the board wouldn't back me up.
SubTotal: MUST HAVES	1	

WOULDN'T IT BE NICE Questions:		COMMENTS
Background in Finance?	X	CPA with great connections to big business donors
Interest in PR?		
SubTotal: WOULDN'T IT BE NICE	1	

NEVER IN A MILLION YEARS		COMMENTS
Angry!!	X	Even though he talked about giving people freedom, when it came to real examples, he was angry and critical.
SubTotal: NEVER IN A MILLION YEARS	-1	

GUT HUNCH	-1	He made me feel uneasy, like he wasn't going to trust anyone

TOTAL SCORE	0	

Scoring the Answers

Be Consistent

Some groups like to determine BEFORE the interview if there are "deal breaker questions" - the question that will make or break whether or not a candidate is recommended for appointment to the board. Other groups like to determine before the interview how many checkmarks they want to see for someone to be thought of as a "good" candidate, especially in the "Must Have" category. And some groups just add them up and see what they've got.

Regardless of your approach, when the interview is over and you add up the check marks to see how many of your criteria each candidate has, remember to be consistent across all candidates in this final step.

The Gut Hunch

In all this calculating and assigning points, one thing is missing - the gut hunch.

While I wouldn't bet the whole farm on a gut hunch, I would certainly take one of two similar candidates based on that gut. Gut hunches move the world forward, and there is a place for them in this process.

Was one of the candidates so enthusiastic that they had already volunteered for a committee? Was the click so good with one that you all instantly started planning a great fundraising event together?

Was one of the candidates so untrusting that the whole room started to agree that maybe you need to investigate your CFO for fraud? Were they so negative you couldn't wait for them to leave or at least stop talking?

At the bottom of the page, under all your questions, put a space for gut hunches. **This is the only place that will get a numerical score, rather than just a check mark.** If your gut says, "This guy is GREAT!" then give him a **+1**, which will add one point to his total score. If your gut says, "Never in a million years," then give him a **-1**, and subtract one point from his score. Your gut has real value here, and it is important to fill in the comment space to note why.

Scoring

First, add up the sub-total of "Must-Have's". These are the most important. You can use these to initially measure candidates against each other.

Then add up the sub-total for the "Wouldn't It Be Nice's". Remember that these marks may put a good candidate over the top, but they can't substitute for those "Must Have" qualifications. A bossy jerk who happens to have money will be a lousy board member.

Which brings us to the last two items. If you've made any notes in this area, add up the "Never in a Million Years" list. GIVE THIS SCORE A NEGATIVE NUMBER.

Then add in your gut hunch - it will either be positive or negative.

And tally away! Add up those check marks, and see who your next board members will be!

A Word About This Calculated Approach

Yes, this is a very calculated approach. Some organizations choose to do even more than this - they get references from prospects, and they check on those references. Some choose to do less.

You don't have to do any of this - you can choose to simply meet with the candidates and talk about the board in a more general way - more of a getting to know you exercise.

The problem arises when you have more than one candidate for a board seat (which is desirable for ultimate board performance). Then, if you don't have a formal interview process, you will be basing your decisions on the subjective views of whoever was in the room for the interview - whether or not they "liked" the person. That process doesn't allow you to determine which of the candidates would really do the best job for the board, and doesn't let you convey that to the rest of the board (including and especially the person who nominated him/her!)

And that's the bottom line. It's a job. Get the best people, and the board will do amazing things for the organization.

Don't Settle for Less

A word of caution. Once you've gone through this whole process, you will be inclined to feel you have to pick somebody, even if none of the candidates measure up.

But if none of the candidates has the level of qualifications you are seeking, you don't have to choose anyone!

Would you like to be stuck with the guy in the sample form on page 92, just because he was better than three other bad choices?

The point of this whole process is to improve the quality of your board members, so that your board and your organization can function at their best. Do you want to go through this whole process, only to shortchange that?

If none of the candidates is the best person for the job, **DON'T FILL THAT SEAT UNTIL THE RIGHT ONE COMES ALONG!**

And if some of those candidates will make great volunteers or committee members or honorary board members, find a place for them in your organization where they CAN make a difference.

A STORY

Getting to Know Each Other

We were in the early stages of instituting a completely new recruitment process with the Abalone Group. They didn't have a whole pool of candidates yet, just their very first candidate to go through their new process. The Board Development Committee was excited.

They were in the process of creating an introductory brochure when a candidate was approached by a current board member about being on the board. So they provided the draft of the brochure to the candidate, with their apologies and explanations about the process being brand new. The candidate was good natured about being the guinea pig.

The Board Development Committee split up the assignments. One of them arranged a tour of the facility while two others set up the interview. They didn't have time to pre-write questions, but they had already established criteria for what they wanted in a board member. They decided to invent their questions on the spot.

The day of the interview, the committee happened to be meeting on another matter. So we all sat waiting for the two interviewers to report back.

We had never seen them so excited - like they'd been on a first date! They had obviously clicked with this new person, to the point where they had together figured out which committee the candidate would benefit the most. The person matched all their criteria, and they had had a terrific time together. They actually looked forward to working together.

By the time the committee recommended this person for the board, they knew him well. Unlike situations where the only one who knows the candidate is the one who proposed him/her for membership, this candidate could comfortably be recommended by the whole committee.

The energy created through this process was tremendous. And upon being voted onto the board, the new board member already had a head start on making a terrific contribution to the group.

As an aside, this organization recently had an annual audit by a major funder. The funder was thrilled with their Board Introductory Brochure, saying repeatedly throughout the day, "We've never seen anything like this!" The auditors took a copy to share with other agencies, and gave the group extra points in their evaluation just for having it!

"We are what we repeatedly do. Excellence, therefore, is not an act but a habit."

Aristotle

Step 5:
Preparing the New Board Member to Govern

"What Don't We Know?"

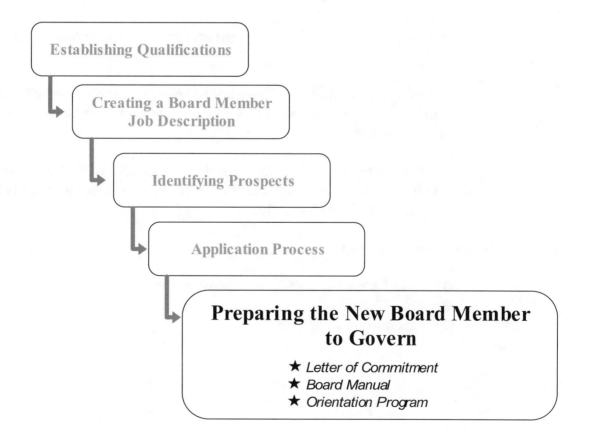

Establishing Qualifications

Creating a Board Member Job Description

Identifying Prospects

Application Process

Preparing the New Board Member to Govern

★ *Letter of Commitment*
★ *Board Manual*
★ *Orientation Program*

OVERVIEW:
Preparing the New Board Member to Govern

If your board is like most boards, your new board members will sit quietly, absorbing the culture and trying to see where they fit in. Sometimes new board members don't feel comfortable in really participating until they've been at it for a whole year!

We have worked with a board whose members, after a year of service, still had never toured the facility.

We have worked with a board whose staff gave a presentation to 'update' the board on the services they provide, while old time board members whispered to each other, "I never knew we did half those things!"

We've given quizzes to boards on the organization's level of service, budget and other critical pieces of information, where 3/4 of the board failed.

How can we expect these folks to govern and make informed decisions?

Now we already know that your new board members won't just sit around waiting to fit in, because your application process has them ready to rock and roll as soon as they're voted on.

And so in this section, you'll find some tools to make their transition to board member a smooth one, ensuring that their initial enthusiasm is quickly converted into participation and productivity.

The tools described in this section include:

- ✪ Board Member Letter of Commitment
- ✪ Board Manual
- ✪ Orientation Program

★★★★★★★★★

CHAPTER 15

★★★★★★★★★

Board Member Letter of Commitment

Many boards require that board members sign a commitment letter, formally accepting the responsibility of governing the organization.

The commitment letter can be as broad-brushed as a single paragraph: "I have read the board manual and know what's expected of me."

It can be as specific as "I understand that there will be one 2-hour board meeting per month, and 2 committee meetings per month (2 hours each), for a total of 6 hours per month. I further understand that there may be planning sessions or other board events that will require my time. I therefore commit to providing XYZ Agency with at least 100 hours in the year, to participate in these board-related activities."

A typical letter of commitment will, in part, follow your job description and may include:

★ Commit to the vision, mission and values of the organization

★ Commit to act within established policies and bylaws

★ Time commitment - not just for regular board meetings, but committee meetings, special meetings, etc.

★ Commit to act in the best interest of the organization, putting the organization's interests above their own

★ Commit to hold confidential matters in confidence

★ Commit to prepare for, attend and participate in meetings

★ Commit to participate in board functions such as fundraisers, tours or other activities

★ Commit to participate in at least one committee

★ Specific reiterations of policies governing board member behavior, such as attendance policies, etc.

Attached to the Letter of Commitment should be a separate statement disclosing any conflicts of interest.* This statement should be updated annually by every member of the board, not just new members, to

a) disclose any new financial relationships that may affect the organization,

and

b) remind board members of the organization's conflict of interest policies and their importance.

In addition to providing the board member with the message that you are asking for a serious commitment, the letter can be used to directly prescribe board member behavior. If they sign the letter of commitment and then can't / won't abide the rules to which they've lent their signature, the board then has grounds for their removal.

★★ *We strongly recommend that your conflict of interest disclosure statement, as well as the section of bylaws to which it directly pertains, be drafted by an attorney who specializes in NonProfit law, as the IRS has specific standards for conflict of interest and private inurement, and violation carries severe penalties.*

Sample Letter of Commitment

The following sample letter can be used as a guide. Your board will want to substitute items that are particularly important to your organization, as well as language that may be more appropriate. You may wish to have your attorney review this document, to see if anything pertinent to your organization has been left out.

If your organization has a code of ethics or statement of values, you may want to attach it to your letter of commitment, and reference it in the document.

A conflict of interest disclosure, prepared by your attorney, should be attached to this document, for separate signature.

PLEASE NOTE:
This sample letter of commitment errs on the side of direct and strict. You may wish to make yours more lenient or more friendly. The form and tone may change, but the intent is what is important - that they are committing to help your organization be the best it can be, and that they are willing to do what it takes to accomplish that.

LETTER OF COMMITMENT

I, _____, agree to serve on the _____ Board of Directors. As a member of this board, I hereby:

a)   Commit to act in the best interests of the vision and mission of the organization, and to uphold the values of the organization.

b)   Commit to put the organization's best interests above my own.

c)   Commit to act in accordance with the bylaws and policies of the organization.

d)   Commit to participate in at least one committee.

e)   Commit to prepare for, attend and participate in board and committee meetings.

f)   Commit to attend orientation and other board education functions.

g)   Commit to participate in board functions, such as fundraisers, tours and other activities.

h)   Commit to hold confidential matters in confidence.

i)   Understand that the board meets __ times per month for ____ hours; that committees meet ____ times per month for ____ hours; and that there may be additional special meetings in any given month. I understand that I am therefore committing approximately ____ hours per month to participating in these meetings.

I understand that the role of Board Member is a critical role for this organization, and therefore I understand that my failure to live up to these commitments may result in my removal from the board.

As agreed this ___ day of _____, 200_,

_____   _____
Signature   Print Name

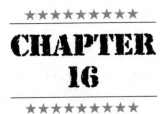

CHAPTER 16

Board Manual

Every board manual we've seen is the same in one way - most board members rarely use it. Yet most boards think the manual could be a very useful tool.

So how do we convert that binder from boat anchor to a resource you can't live without?

Ask the board

The first step is to ask your board what uses they perceive for the manual, and how it could serve those purposes. Brainstorming questions might include

★ What are potential uses for the board manual at board meetings? At committee meetings?

★ What do you use the book for now?

★ How would you use it if the information were different? What different information would be useful?

★ What is in the book now that we don't need?

★ What works well about the current book?

★ What doesn't work about the current book?

Board Manual Items to Consider

The following is a list of items that may be helpful to include in your board manual. It is offered to assist with your brainstorming, and NOT as a "Must Have" list. When you begin to add things to the manual, remember that it will get heavier and heavier to carry - and the more unwieldy it gets, the less it will be used.

The best approach is to ask your board what they perceive they'll need, and to start small, adding things only as you need them.

Possible items for inclusion in Board Manual:

★ Current Board of Directors List, with addresses, phone and email addresses

★ Committee list with "mission statements" for each committee

★ Specific information based on committee membership of that individual board member

★ Bylaws

★ Board policies broken down by category - finance, etc.

★ Board member job description

★ Brief overview of organization's purpose, mission, history

★ Annual board calendar

★ Organizational chart

★ Annual report

★ Annual budget

★ Strategic plan

★ Certified audit

★ Glossary of common terms, list of commonly used names (funding sources, industry terms, etc.)

★ Applicable phone numbers for staff (direct line for ED, perhaps, including home phone).

CHAPTER 17

Orientation Program

No, sending your new board member home to study your new-and-improved board manual does NOT constitute an orientation program!

Orientation serves one essential purpose - to give new board members enough knowledge about the organization and their role in it, so that each one can hit the ground running. The better the orientation program, the faster your new board members can be participating in governing the organization.

There are two steps to creating an effective orientation program:

1. Determine what information needs to be conveyed
2. Determine the most effective way to convey that information

When creating orientation programs, we tend to get that order reversed. We head right for the toolbox, determining that "we need a video," or "we need a tour," and then trying to figure out what the content should be. After all, the tools are the fun part!

Let the content guide the tools. First establish what folks need to learn. Then figure out the best way for them to learn that.

Orientation Program - Content

The easiest way to determine what information should be in your orientation program is to ask your board and CEO.

Board

★ What do you wish you had known when you started on the board, to help you make more informed decisions?

★ What information do you feel you are lacking even now?

CEO

★ What areas of the organization do you feel the board doesn't understand well enough to make informed decisions?

These will be the topics your orientation program should cover.

Topics that often come up in these conversations include:

★ Board rules and policies / how the board functions

★ Information about the organization / history / programs

★ Financial information
- ★ Specific to the organization
- ★ How to understand finances in general

★ Role of the Board / Role of each board member / Role of each committee

Once you start discussing these issues, you will find all kinds of areas that folks have kept quiet about, figuring, "I must be the only one who doesn't know that." This will be especially apparent in the area of finances, where truly very few people feel comfortable, but most just nod along. How many of your board members really understand your financials? How many understand what implications they have for the organization?

Discussion of your orientation program will be a great eye-opener for the whole board. It is a great exercise for their awareness of what it takes to really do their job well. Usually these discussions are energizing and revealing - boards love this topic!

Once you have created the orientation program, you will probably want the whole board to go through that program. In our experience, once they've gone through the exercise of voicing what they wish they'd known, they all WANT to go through that first program!

We frequently recommend that every board member go through orientation every year to two years. Programs and services change, and sometimes we need a reminder of some of the things that DON'T change as well. Staying informed is part of the responsibility of being a board member - how else can you effectively govern?

PREPARING THE NEW BOARD MEMBER OT GOVERN

BRAINST✪RM - What Must a Board Member Know
to Make Informed Decisions?

BOARD	• *What do you wish you had known when you started on the board, to help you make more informed decisions?* • *What information do you feel you are lacking even now?*

CEO	• *What areas of the organization do you feel the board doesn't understand well enough to make informed decisions?*

© 2001 Help 4 NonProfits & Tribes
www.help4nonprofits.com

Orientation Program: How to Convey that Information

There are a few tried and true methods of getting information to new board members in an efficient and effective way. Making good use of their time will be critical, because board members are usually busy people. The following are good methods for providing a ton of information in a time efficient manner:

- **Half-day orientation sessions**, with staff and board as teachers of the various topics. A tour of the facility is often a good wrap-up to the session, even if they toured before joining the board. The first tour was to get them interested in the organization. This tour is to solidify and make real the information they've just learned.

- **Orientation Video**. A video may replace a live session. Or it may be used at home, to augment what they learn in a live session. Or it may even be shown during the live session, as an introduction to many of the concepts. Because of its flexibility, a good board orientation video is often a handy tool.

- **Mentoring Program**. This is a great way to transfer knowledge from a more seasoned board member to a newer one. It does not replace the video or teaching session, but extends the learning into however many months is reasonable for your organization. Having a mentor creates an instant "friend" inside the organization - someone who can tell you the real skinny, rather than your having to find it out on your own.

    Being chosen as a mentor should be an honor to aspire to. The Board Development committee would be advised to choose as mentors only those board members it trusts not to be catty or otherwise troublesome, as bad information can be passed along in this process just as easily as good information. "I hate so-and-so; he's a real jerk," is not the kind of information that is best spread to new board members!

Mentoring is one of the most effective tools for bringing new board members up to speed on the kinds of things you just can't learn in a class - the culture of the organization, expectations, etc.

★★★★★★★★★

CHAPTER 18

★★★★★★★★★

The Last Step - Put Them to Work

Once a board member has gone through orientation and is ready to participate, put them to work - fast! All your careful recruitment and all this new board member's enthusiasm will be wasted if there is nothing for them to sink their teeth into once they are voted in.

Provide them with an array of activities and committees from which to choose, and let them start helping the board and the organization now!

What Don't We Know?

At the Animal Center's retreat, the Executive Director thought it would be interesting to devote the lunch hour to staff updates on the various programs the center provided. Each program was given 10 minutes to update the board.

That lunch hour changed their lives. What the ED thought was an update was really new information to most of the board members, regardless of their tenure on the board. After the break, one board member asked, "If we don't know such a basic thing as the programs the center offers, what else do we not know?" And they spent the rest of the afternoon thinking about just that.

One of the newer board members mentioned that she felt lost not knowing everyone's name. And the group couldn't believe they'd never thought of such a simple thing as name tags, to smooth the transition for new board members.

One of the veteran board members said, "I hate to say this, but since we're confessing... I don't understand a thing about the financials. I know I should, but I just don't do anything at work where I would learn this stuff. So when we talk about the financials, I just look at my papers or play with my pen." That one comment unleashed such a flood of me-too's that the board decided to create an ongoing financial education program for board members, requiring them to pass a test to show they understand the types of financial information they were legally charged with overseeing.

The day went on like that, with one confessing what they didn't know and getting immediate support from others who were in the same boat. By day's end, they had crafted a program for board orientation and continuing board improvement, all in one!

Equally as important, though, was the experience of sharing what they had previously kept hidden - all the things they didn't know. That afternoon brought this board together in ways no team-building exercise ever could have. And it put them on the road to responsible governance.

Afterwords

"The Board is Responsible for Creating The Future, Not Minding the Shop."
John Carver

We mentioned in the Introduction that recruitment and orientation alone will not make your board the best it can be. The following tips and resources are intended to guide you to improvement in other critical areas of board performance.

★ Defining the role of the board

★ Measuring board members' performance and removal of board members

★ What to do with individuals who aren't board material

★ A free service worth its weight in gold

CHAPTER 19

Clearly Defining the Role of the Board

Although you have written a job description for individual board members, one of the biggest problems facing boards is that the board as a whole is uncertain about its own role within the organization. When the board doesn't understand its job, individual board members cannot succeed, job description or no.

To determine if your board needs help in this area, ask yourself the following questions:

★ What percentage of time at each board meeting is spent talking about things that have already happened (staff reports, financial reports, etc.)?

★ What percentage of time is spent talking about the impact the organization will make on the community?

★ **True or false:** Our board discusses such important matters for guiding the organization that the organization would have no overall direction without those discussions.

★ When you review the budget, how do you know whether or not you should approve it?

★ Of the total budget for your organization, which items were discussed at length? Do any of those items comprise less than 1% of your budget (on a $1million budget, that would be $10,000 or less)? What percentage of the budget was passed without comment? Why?

★ **True or false**: Our board discusses such important matters for the future of our community that I feel horrible missing a single meeting.

How many of the following would you agree with?

★ Our board spends a great deal of time on trivial items.

★ We receive reams of paper before each board meeting, but I don't think anyone really reads it all.

★ The staff complains that the board micromanages, but we're just doing our job.

★ Our board discusses issues, but in the end we pretty much approve whatever the staff requests.

★ We haven't done a review of our executive director in at least 2 years.

★ We review our executive director every year, but we have no quantifiable criteria by which to measure his/her performance.

★ I've been on this board for a little over a year, and I'm finally getting a sense of how I can contribute.

★ I've been on this board for a little over a year, and I'm STILL not really sure where I fit in.

And finally, the question we noted back in the Introduction, per that study cited in the Wall Street Journal:

If your board was abducted by aliens, would the
organization notice they were gone?
Would anyone pay to get them back?

If you read the items on the preceding page and chuckled or winced (or both) at most of the questions, don't feel bad. Board functions are generally the last area to be improved as NonProfits grow.

When a board is functioning well, it plays a pivotal role in guiding the future of the organization and delivering results to the community. At that point in the board's maturity, a strong recruitment process will continue to strengthen your board.

However, when a board is functioning poorly, recruitment will not help make the board better, regardless of how good that recruitment process is. It is hard to attract, train and retain new board members when the existing board is confused, uncertain, tentative. In addition, a dysfunctional board can, and often will turn off those recruits you've worked so hard to cultivate, leading to higher board turnover and potentially creating an appearance of instability in the community.

The fact that you care enough about your board's performance to have read and/or used this workbook means that you are on the path to improving that performance.

CHAPTER 20

Measuring Board Members' Performance

We give our employees periodic evaluations because the review process helps them to improve, and because it helps us to notice when the employee just isn't cutting it. At one end of the spectrum, evaluations help us get back to what's important. At the other end, they help create a paper trail.

There are various tools we can use to evaluate board members. The most basic are bylaws and policies. More elaborate self-assessment tools exist, but if you don't have solid bylaws and policies, there's no point in reaching for the fancy tools.

Bylaws and Policies: Putting Teeth Into Your Job Description

You've started your recruitment process by listing the qualifications you desire in a board member, and you've created the job description by combining those criteria with the requirements of the job itself. A board member must be a team player. A board member must be available to attend meetings. A board member must be the type of person to put the best interests of the organization first.

Bylaws and policies allow you to reinforce those good behaviors by outlining the consequences for NOT behaving according to those policies.

And that is critical for a successful board.

Bylaws

Bylaws are the organization's basic legal framework. They define the organization's internal structure and external purpose. The bylaws are not the policies and procedures manual, but they are its foundation. As such, they are the final word in what is permissible.

For that reason, bylaws are usually fairly general, to allow the organization the flexibility to change how they might interpret and implement those bylaws over time.

As the final word in what the board can and cannot do, bylaws delineate how a board member is voted onto the board, and as such, they govern under what circumstances that board member can be removed from the board. That could be a mechanism as simple as term limits, or, in the worst cases, it could be the forcible removal of a board member for impropriety.

But just like the bylaws govern how someone can be added to your board, it is the bylaws that will govern whether and how you can remove someone from the board. If those provisions do not exist in your bylaws, then you have no recourse if someone needs to go - you have no legal grounds for removing them.

Bylaws Legal Tip

Bylaws are a legal document. Do not adjust your bylaws without the counsel of an attorney who specializes in NonProfit Law.

Also, as a legal document, bylaws are governed by the laws of the state in which the organization is incorporated. And so the bylaws of an organization in Nebraska may not meet the needs of an organization in New York, and may certainly not meet the needs of an organization operating outside the United States. An attorney who specializes in NonProfit law is invaluable in making sure your organization navigates the law appropriately.

Policies

Policies are the day-to-day rules by which the board governs and the CEO manages the organization. Policies may change over time, to adapt to circumstances. They can be as general or as based in minutiae as the board feels they need to be to get the job done. Whereas the bylaws will provide the legal mechanism for removing a board member, the policies will determine what is appropriate and inappropriate behavior, upon which those decisions for removal will eventually be based.

Are Your Bylaws and Policies Doing the Job?

To determine if your bylaws and policies are adequate to protect the board in the event a board member isn't cutting it, ask yourself the following questions:

★ What happens to a board member who chronically misses meetings? Does it make a difference if those absences are excused or unexcused?

★ Does your board have problems getting a quorum? Do you ever have to cancel or postpone meetings due to a lack of quorum?

★ Does your board have a particular board member who is disruptive? Are there rules to discourage this behavior? Are those rules applied consistently to all board members?

★ If a board member divulges confidential information, do you have policies that provide for a reprimand or other consequences?

★ If a disgruntled employee decides to get even by joining the board, are there policies that would allow the board to gracefully decline their application?

★ Does your board periodically review its bylaws and policies to see that they are still applicable? Are they reviewed to determine if these rules are applied consistently to all board members?

A Word About Enforcing Bylaws and Policies

The following words have been stated throughout this workbook, but they bear repeating.

Bylaws and policies are ONLY enforceable if they are enforced consistently and evenhandedly. Just because you have a rule doesn't mean you can suddenly decide to use it after years of letting things slide.

If you create rules, enforce them consistently. Otherwise it's like not having any rules at all.

Removing Board Members

Removing board members is the biggest problem boards DON'T face. Boards may willingly face all their other problems, but this one they ignore - sometimes for years.

> *Joe is a HORRIBLE board member. He is disruptive. He doesn't show up for meetings for months at a time, and when he does show up, he complains. He goes against policy. He angers the staff.*
>
> *How long has Joe been like this?*
>
> *Years.*

We've come full circle, back to the very beginning of this workbook, where we talked about "The Thing That Wouldn't Leave." Joe was recruited onto the board and there he stays. And while the best thing would have been to have never invited him at all, that's no longer an option.

It's time to make "The Thing That Wouldn't Leave" go home.

The options available to your board will depend on whether or not you have policies in place that permit you to remove Joe. If there are no policies, they will need to be created before Joe can be escorted to the door.

If, however, you do already have policies, then it's time to do the hard thing and remove Joe from the board.

Oh, this is the very hardest thing we face as a board. It is like firing one of our own - not a subordinate, but a peer. And it makes everyone uncomfortable - no one wants to play the heavy, and most of us would rather have a tooth pulled than face confrontation.

But we're not talking here about political issues or someone who just doesn't fit in. We are talking about someone going directly and blatantly counter to policy - policy that your board has established so that you can continue to bring the organization forward. And the only way your policies will ever deter bad behavior is if they include consequences, and those consequences are consistently applied.

Your board's reason for being is to maintain continuity and provide results on behalf of the community. Your board is all about the future of the organization - about moving forward. Joe is pulling the organization **BACKWARDS**. He needs to go.

There are so many ways to finesse Joe's removal from the board (including warnings, etc.) that they could be the topic of an entire workbook. What matters is that you have:

★ Policies against which to measure board members' performance;

★ Bylaws that give you the legal authority to remove a board member; and

★ The organizational backbone to follow through.

Resources to Help Your Board

The following additional resources may be helpful as you expand your board's capabilities.

www.Help4NonProfits.com

Our website is an ever-growing compendium of resources to assist you as you move your board forward - articles, links, downloadable forms. Stroll through the aisles of our NonProfit bookstore to find books that will completely turn around your thinking when it comes to the role of a governing board. *www.Help4NonProfits.com*

John Carver's "Boards That Make A Difference" and its companion, "Reinventing Your Board"

Speaking of turning around your thinking, Carver will certainly do that. Although he is pretty insistent that his is an all-or-nothing approach, you will find that you can, in fact, go slowly, implementing those ideas that make the most sense to your organization. A must for boards that are trying to clarify their role in the organization. *www.carvergovernance.com*

The National Center for Nonprofit Boards

The NCNB is dedicated to increasing the effectiveness of NonProfit organizations by strengthening their boards of directors. Through its programs and services, NCNB provides solutions and tools to improve board performance. Their membership materials, as well as their books and their website provide a great deal of information to improve your board. *www.ncnb.org*

Internet NonProfit Center

A project of the Evergreen State Society of Seattle, Washington. Information for and about NonProfit organizations in the United States. Their NonProfit FAQ (Frequently Asked Questions, for those who aren't used to Internet lingo) is one of the best sources for basic NonProfit management information. *www.nonprofit-info.org/npofaq/*

Management Assistance Program for NonProfits

Another free on-line library with articles on every topic imaginable regarding NonProfit management. *www.mapnp.org/library/index.html*

★★★★★★★★★

CHAPTER 21

★★★★★★★★★

What to Do with Someone Who is NOT Board Material

At some point in the recruitment process, you are bound to find someone who doesn't have what it takes to be a board member, but who has talents and skills the agency could put to use. Just because they are not right for the board doesn't mean there is no place for their willingness to serve!

The solution is to find a role for this person where their value can be put to good use, and where their seeming "negatives" can be turned into positives.

★ A risk-averse naysayer may make a great committee member in a search for a new building, critically evaluating various properties and reporting back on potential pitfalls. Or that same person might be of great assistance in helping with risk management issues, on a committee and NOT on the board.

★ Or what about someone who has been a long-time volunteer, who now wants to be on the board - but who doesn't measure up? Her knowledge of the organization from the volunteers' perspective might make her the perfect choice to help create volunteer training programs.

There are lots of places these folks can excel. They just shouldn't be on the board.

★ For people who want to be on the board to just lend their name, you might form an Honorary Board of folks whose names will be helpful.

★ For people who want to be on the board to raise money or perform some other very narrow task where they can lend their expertise, you might put them on a committee or have them volunteer.

★ For people who want to be on the board to help out, but won't attend meetings, you might create an advisory council of folks who can help with connections and advice.

And when you find those who really want to govern, to help move the organization towards a big picture vision for the future, THOSE ARE THE ONES YOU WANT ON YOUR BOARD!

CHAPTER 22

A Free Tip Worth Its Weight in Gold

NonProfit staff have access to all kinds of professional education. They receive flyers and newsletters in the mail. They read NonProfit newspapers like the Chronicle of Philanthropy. They talk to other NonProfit professionals all day long.

Board members usually get little or none of this. Frequently the only access board members have to this kind of information is what staff gives them. And they rarely talk about the nitty gritty of what it means to be a board member, even with other members of the board.

Now there is a great tool to keep you informed and aware of the issues that affect boards. It's called *Charity Channel*, and it's FREE!

Charity Channel is a series of moderated Internet discussion groups centered around NonProfit issues. It is a question and answer forum, a place to air what's bothering you, a place to connect with other board members from all over the country and the world. It provides you with information daily, all via your email.

Charity Channel is an amazing way to learn.

Lurk or participate. Ask or answer or just watch. *Charity Channel* has been hailed by the best in our field as being the single best source of continuing education that exists anywhere for NonProfit leaders, volunteers, employees, board members, and donors - and for those who help NonProfits for a living, such as consultants and attorneys.

Charity Channel has a special list just for Boards, so sign up and be ready to learn a little bit every day. For more information, head to *www.CharityChannel.com*

The End

COMING IN 2002
★★★★★★★★★★★★★★★★★

For a Whole New Way of Looking at
Fund Development
Watch for the Next Book in the
Basic Training 4 NonProfits Workbook Series

Building a Sustainable Organization:
A Step-by-Step, Common Sense Guide

by Hildy Gottlieb

To reserve your copy, head to
www.Help4NonProfits.com
or
call us in the U.S.
at 1-888-787-4433

QUICK ORDER FORM

I would like to order additional copies of

Board Recruitment and Orientation
A Step-by-Step, Common Sense Guide
by Hildy Gottlieb

Order Online:
www.Help4NonProfits.com

Order by Phone:
1-888-787-4433 in the U.S.

Order by Mail: Name: _____

Address: _____

_____

City: _____ State: _____ Zip: _____

Phone: _____

Email: _____

Sales Tax:
Please add 7.5% for Books shipped to Arizona addresses.

Shipping:
U.S. $4.00 for first book and $2.00 for each additional.
International $9.00 for first book and $5.00 for each additional (estimated cost - email us with specifics for final cost.)

Copies Ordered:

Payment Method:
❑ **Check**

Number of Books _____ (@ $17.95) _____

Send To:
Renaissance Press
P.O. Box 13121
Tucson, Arizona 85732 U.S.A.

Sales Tax _____

Shipping _____

❑ **Credit Card**   ❑ Master Card   ❑ Visa

TOTAL _____

Card Number: _____ Exp. _____ / ____

Name on Card: _____

Signature: _____

I understand that I may return the book for a full refund for any reason, no questions asked.